ROAD PRICING AND PROVISION

CHANGED TRAFFIC CONDITIONS AHEAD

ROAD PRICING AND PROVISION

CHANGED TRAFFIC CONDITIONS AHEAD

Edited by Michael de Percy
and John Wanna

Australian
National
University

PRESS

ANU PRESS

the Australia and New Zealand
School of Government

Published by ANU Press
The Australian National University
Acton ACT 2601, Australia
Email: anupress@anu.edu.au

Available to download for free at press.anu.edu.au

ISBN (print): 9781760462307
ISBN (online): 9781760462314

WorldCat (print): 1045638049
WorldCat (online): 1045638056

DOI: 10.22459/RPP.07.2018

Cover design and layout by ANU Press

Contents

Section 1: Introduction

Section 2: Long-term planning

Section 3: Road pricing

Section 4: Turning theory into practice

Contributors

Gary Banks AO is a Professorial Fellow at the Melbourne Institute for Applied Economic and Social Research. He was chief executive and dean of the Australia and New Zealand School of Government (ANZSOG) until January 2017 and chairman of the Productivity Commission from its inception in 1998 until 2013. He is also Chair of the Regulatory Policy Committee of the Organisation for Economic Co-operation and Development (OECD).

Philip Davies is Chief Executive Officer of Infrastructure Australia. Previously, Philip led AECOM's Infrastructure Advisory business in the Asia-Pacific and served as a director of Transport for London (TfL), where he played a key role in the planning and implementation of congestion charging in central London, and the establishment of London's transport control centre. Philip is a chartered professional engineer, a Fellow of Engineers Australia and a Fellow of the Australian Institute of Company Directors.

Michael de Percy is Senior Lecturer in Political Science at the University of Canberra, Academic Fellow of the Institute for Governance and Policy Analysis, a chartered member of the Chartered Institute of Logistics and Transport and a graduate of the Royal Military College, Duntroon.

Brendan Lyon is Chief Executive Officer of Infrastructure Partnerships Australia. Previously, he served on the board of Transport for NSW (formerly the NSW Department of Transport), the Infrastructure Regulation Advisory Committee of the Australian Competition and Consumer Commission (ACCC), the federal government's Infrastructure Finance Working Group and the expert reference panel overseeing the study of high-speed rail.

Alex Robson is Director of the Economic Policy Analysis Program at Griffith University. Alex has more than 20 years experience as an economist in various roles at the Commonwealth Treasury, Deloitte Access Economics and Concept Economics in Canberra, and as a consultant to various state and federal departments and the OECD.

Teik Soon Looi is Dean of the Land Transport Authority (LTA) Academy, Singapore, and Director of Future Mobility and Industry Development in the LTA. He was previously the director in charge of public transport policies and served as secretary of the Public Transport Council from 2006 to 2009.

Marion Terrill is Transport Program Director at the Grattan Institute. She is a leading policy analyst and her experience ranges from authoring parts of the 2010 Henry review to leading the design and development of the MyGov account. She has provided expert analysis and advice on labour market policy for the Australian Government, the Business Council of Australia and at The Australian National University.

John Wanna holds the Sir John Bunting Chair of Public Administration at the Research School of Social Sciences at The Australian National University and is Director of Research for the Australia and New Zealand School of Government (ANZSOG).

Peter Winder is Director of McGredy Winder & Co., an Auckland-based consulting firm. In recent years, Peter facilitated and project managed the work of the Consensus Building Group and the Independent Advisory Board on Alternative Transport Funding for Auckland. Peter was previously chief executive of Local Government New Zealand, director of transport and then chief executive of the Auckland Regional Council. He is one of four commissioners running the Kaipara District Council and Chairman of the Manukau Institute of Technology.

Abbreviations

AAA	Australian Automobile Association
ABARE	Australian Bureau of Agricultural and Resource Economics
ABRD	Australian Bicentennial Road Development
ABS	Australian Bureau of Statistics
AC	average cost
ACCC	Australian Competition and Consumer Commission
ALS	Area Licensing Scheme
ANZSOG	Australia and New Zealand School of Government
ATAP	Auckland Transport Alignment Project
ATO	Australian Taxation Office
AV	autonomous vehicle
BITRE	Bureau of Infrastructure, Transport and Regional Economics
BSEP	Bus Service Enhancement Program
BTE	Bureau of Transport Economics
CBD	central business district
CBR	Commonwealth Bureau of Roads
CEO	chief executive officer
COAG	Council of Australian Governments
CoE	Certificate of Entitlement
CPI	consumer price index
EPAC	Economic Planning Advisory Commission
ERP	Electronic Road Pricing

FIRS	Federal Interstate Registration Scheme
GDP	gross domestic product
GFC	Global Financial Crisis
GNSS	Global Navigation Satellite System
GPS	Global Positioning System
GST	goods and services tax
HDB	Housing Development Board
HVNL	Heavy Vehicle National Law
IPART	Independent Pricing and Regulatory Tribunal
JTC	Jurong Town Corporation
LoS	level of service
LPG	liquid petroleum gas
LRT	Light Rail Transit
LTA	Land Transport Authority (Singapore)
LTMP	Land Transport Master Plan
MB	marginal benefit
MC	marginal cost
MRT	mass rapid transit
NCP	National Competition Policy
NSW	New South Wales
NZTA	New Zealand Transport Agency
OECD	Organisation for Economic Co-operation and Development
PPP	public–private partnership
RACV	Royal Automobile Club of Victoria
RFID	radio-frequency identification
TfL	Transport for London
URA	Urban Redevelopment Authority
URUC	universal road user charging

Figures

Tables

Foreword

Ian Harper[1]

Road pricing was not a major focus of the 2015 Competition Policy Review (Harper et al. 2015). Only one of its 56 recommendations related to road pricing, yet the subject attracted the largest number of submissions of any issue before the review panel—that is, if each of the numerous copies of the same one-page leaflet forwarded to the secretariat from people staunchly opposed to road pricing was counted as a separate submission!

Road pricing raises hackles. The authors of the one-page leaflet asserted that 'our roads belong to the people, not the government' and 'our roads have been paid for already—we shouldn't have to pay for them again'. People might have said the same of dams and water mains, or even electricity poles and wires, but they did not. There is something about paying to use public roads that infuriates people far more than paying for water, electricity or gas, even when these utilities are also in public ownership.

Yet the principles for efficiently allocating scarce resources (public or private) to road transport are no different from those applying to other networked utilities such as reticulated water, electricity or gas. That is why the Competition Policy Review included a discussion of road pricing along with the pricing and regulation of other infrastructure.

Road pricing is not a new idea, nor is it untried elsewhere in the world. In fact, the arguments in favour of road pricing are sound, well understood and not especially hard to articulate, as the various chapters of this book

---

1   Ian Harper chaired the Competition Policy Review that reported to the Australian Government in March 2015. He is a Senior Advisor to Deloitte Access Economics and a board member of the Reserve Bank of Australia.

amply demonstrate. Furthermore, technological developments have all but eliminated technical obstacles that have frustrated road pricing advocates for decades. Yet the prospect of treating access to and use of public roads similarly to energy, communication and water reticulation networks seems a distant one. Or is this view too pessimistic?

Alongside the heat generated by the review panel's discussion of road pricing, there was also light. At least one high-profile talkback radio host took me to task in an interview about road pricing, but was discomfited when I asked how sensible it would be for the government to pay for electricity out of general revenue and then just allow people to use as much of it as they wanted. He saw quite quickly that this would result in waste and inefficiency, but it had never occurred to him that roads are funded and allocated in exactly this way.

Since the release of the review's final report in 2015, there have been other reports canvassing different aspects of road pricing, some of which are mentioned in this book. The general tenor of public discussion, meanwhile, has been curious and intrigued rather than outraged, as far as I have observed, encouraged by public support for road pricing offered by motorists' associations, public transport enthusiasts and other road users.

So is road pricing an idea whose time has finally come? The advent of electric vehicles raises the prospect of some users evading even the pretence of a user charge in the form of the fuel excise levy. The fact that these users may be among the wealthier echelons of the community adds urgency to the issue and recasts road pricing as potentially progressive rather than regressive in its impact on income distribution.

Furthermore, the widening application of data analytics is familiarising people with a closer relationship between their behaviour and what they pay for a service. If car insurance premiums, for example, become more sensitive to the time and location of travel, road conditions and congestion levels, as well as driver behaviour, how easy would it be to calibrate a road user charge into the insurance premium? And might not this be encouraged by governments willing to offer a rebate of vehicle registration fees or fuel excise in accordance with users' acceptance of time and distance-based charges for road use? As the so-called sharing economy encourages people to think of assets as streams of services for which they can pay or, alternatively, be paid, again, how natural would it be to package the services provided by the road together with those provided by the vehicle?

My sense is that the ground is shifting for advocates of road pricing. As the various chapters of this timely volume make clear, the academic and policy cases in favour of road pricing are well established. Hand-wringing about the lack of political will to implement this overdue reform—also evident in this book—is understandable, but I wonder whether it isn't also misplaced.

The late Sir Harold Knight, former governor of the Reserve Bank of Australia, used to speak of 'catching the policy train' (Uren 2015). One needs one's bags packed and ticket at the ready, since the 'policy train' keeps an irregular timetable and can pull into the station unexpectedly. The chapters in this volume show that our bags are well and truly packed on this issue, and have been for some time. And now there is a slowly rising din of whistling and rattling to be heard. Might that be the road pricing policy train about to pull into the station?

References

Harper, I., Anderson, P., McCluskey, S. and O'Bryan, M. (2015). *Competition Policy Review: Final Report March 2015*. Canberra: Commonwealth of Australia. Available from: competitionpolicyreview.gov.au/files/2015/03/Competition-policy-review-report_online.pdf

Uren, D. (2015). Pragmatism rules in a parliament that finally works. *The Australian*, 24 October. Available from www.theaustralian.com.au/news/inquirer/pragmatism-rules-in-a-parliament-that-finally-works/news-story/f4c29cfd13acf0c280af72e185fa11a7 (accessed 14 July 2018).

Preface: The importance of road pricing

Mike Mrdak[1]

I have often noted that one of the great things about transport is that everyone has an opinion but very few people have all of the facts. In addition to facilitating policy debate and educating our public sector leaders, the Australia and New Zealand School of Government (ANZSOG) has a critical role in bridging this gap by connecting government with academia and by delivering the research we need to get the solutions that will deliver economic prosperity for our future.

Productivity growth is essential to growing national income, and Australia's transport network has a central role to play in achieving productivity growth. Transport infrastructure is both a stabiliser and a catalyst. It is the lifeblood of our economy, enabling people to connect with jobs and to get goods to market. We are a lucky country in that all the projections indicate that we face a future of growth. But we cannot take this for granted, nor can we afford to be complacent.

In recent years, Australia's population growth has been among the fastest in the developed world. Sydney and Melbourne are each expected to hit a population of 8 million people by 2050 (ABS 2013). All of our major cities are expected to increase their share of the national population. Our cities are where most of our economic activity occurs, but they are also our most significant productivity drains. The scourge of congestion is costing us—$16.5 billion in avoidable costs in 2015–16 and, under current settings, about $30 billion a year by 2030 (BITRE 2015). It is taking people too long to get to and from work. The freight task is also

---

[1] Mike Mrdak AO is Secretary of the Department of Infrastructure and Regional Development.

growing, and is expected to increase by 80 per cent between 2010 and 2030, with the road and rail freight tasks projected to be close to double their 2010 levels by 2030 (BITRE 2014: 8).

We need to reform the way we deliver and pay for transport infrastructure if we are to have sustainable growth, and we know the current model is not sustainable.

The costs of constructing and maintaining our roads continue to rise, as increasing demand adds to the total size of the road network and as the price of engineering and construction services also increases.

Disrupting forces loom for the transport sector as much as for any other industry. Fuel excise revenue has been steadily declining as more fuel-efficient vehicles enter the market. Hybrid and fully electric vehicles will deliver environmental and health benefits, but will further reduce fuel excise revenue.

Partially and fully autonomous vehicles and the rise of ride-sharing services will transform how we travel. These technologies will deliver enormous safety and productivity benefits, but are likely to impact the number of drivers being licensed and vehicles being registered, placing pressure on state and territory revenue streams and local governments' parking coffers.

The current system is also inequitable, with those using the road networks the least subsidising those who derive most benefit from it. Our transport system is underutilised by not matching capacity with demand management in the way that other utilities and service providers do. Essentially, the land transport network has escaped the kind of microeconomic reform that we now take for granted as the most efficient and equitable way to deliver goods and services to markets.

Road pricing is not a new concept—after all, toll roads have existed in Australia since Governor Macquarie established a toll road from Sydney to Parramatta in 1811 (BITRE 2016)—and distance-based charging schemes have been trialled and implemented with varying success overseas. We need look no further than our colleagues in New Zealand to see how distance-based charging mechanisms can be used effectively in the heavy vehicle space, and how sovereign road funds can be ring-fenced for use for reinvestment in the road network.

But how would full market reform of roads look in a federation such as Australia? While we do not yet know the answer to this, I believe we are now at a tipping point, where momentum for reform is beyond doubt. In its responses to the 2016 Australian Infrastructure Plan (Infrastructure Australia 2016) and the 2015 Competition Policy Review (Harper et al. 2015), the Australian Government explicitly supported investigating cost-reflective road pricing as a long-term reform option, and committed to establish a study chaired by an eminent Australian to look into the potential impacts of road pricing reform on road users. The challenges we face in this space are manifold and complex and we still have a long road ahead of us, but with advocacy for reform coming from interest groups as diverse as governments, private transport companies, peak industry bodies, policy think tanks and state motoring clubs, I see more support than ever for changing the way we provide and fund our roads.

This collection of articles from some of the most respected researchers, economists and public sector leaders on road provision and pricing is an invaluable addition to the policy literature. I thank ANZSOG for its initiative in publishing this important collection and commend the articles to everyone with an interest in reforming how we deliver and pay for Australia's roads.

References

Australian Bureau of Statistics (ABS). (2013). *Population Projections Australia*. Cat. no. 3222.0, November. Canberra: ABS. Available from: www.abs. gov.au/AUSSTATS/abs@.nsf/allprimarymainfeatures/5A9C0859C5F50 C30CA25718C0015182F?opendocument

Bureau of Infrastructure, Transport and Regional Economics (BITRE). (2014). *Freightline 1: Australia Freight Transport Overview*. Statistical Report, May. Canberra: Commonwealth of Australia.

Bureau of Infrastructure, Transport and Regional Economics (BITRE). (2015). *Traffic and Congestion Cost Trends for Australian Capital Cities*. Information Sheet 74, November. Canberra: Commonwealth of Australia.

Bureau of Infrastructure, Transport and Regional Economics (BITRE). (2016). *Toll Roads in Australia*. Information Sheet 81, September. Canberra: Commonwealth of Australia.

Harper, I., Anderson, P., McCluskey, S. and O'Bryan, M. (2015). *Competition Policy Review: Final Report March 2015*. Canberra: Commonwealth of Australia. Available from: competitionpolicyreview.gov.au/files/2015/03/Competition-policy-review-report_online.pdf

Infrastructure Australia. (2016). *Australian Infrastructure Plan: Priorities and Reforms for Our Nation's Future*. Sydney: Infrastructure Australia. Available from: infrastructureaustralia.gov.au/policy-publications/publications/Australian-Infrastructure-Plan.aspx

Section 1: Introduction

1

Introduction: Shaping the road pricing and provision debate

Michael de Percy

Road pricing in Australia is shaping up to be an incredibly important policy instrument to change the behaviour of road users and to address the decline in federal fuel excise revenues. The current system of recovering basic costs from road use treats roads as a free-access 'public good' and, aside from toll roads, users do not pay directly for their use of the road network or contribution to congestion. The present system of levy charging (fuel excise and registration charges) has little impact on the *behaviour of road users* and, if the current system remains unchanged, traffic congestion in metropolitan areas is set to cost some $30 billion by 2030 (BITRE 2015). For most non-commercial road users, the cost of using the road network is limited to a fixed annual state government access charge (vehicle registration and licence fee) and the federal fuel excise (currently 40.1 cents per litre). However, since the early 2000s, more fuel-efficient vehicles have reduced fuel usage overall and, consequently, revenue from the fuel excise has been steadily declining (BITRE 2016). Further, the existing user charges (fuel excise and vehicle registration) may discriminate marginally between vehicle types and capacities, but not between *heavy* and *light* users of roads (although heavy users will necessarily pay more fuel excise). Moreover, fuel excise is collected as consolidated revenue by the Commonwealth, and therefore provides no market signals on the demand for particular roads. Consequently, estimates used to direct road provision and maintenance routinely prove to be inaccurate, and often simply increasing the capacity of roads reinforces the behaviour that led to traffic congestion in the first instance.

Other networked infrastructure or utility services provided by governments—such as water, gas, power and telecommunications—have been provided on a user-pays basis since market reforms were introduced beginning in the late 1980s, yet the road network remains the least reformed infrastructure sector. This means that the change in behaviour evidenced in the efficient use of water, home heating, electrical power and telecommunications services—particularly in households—is not evident in our patterns of road use. While user charging has been adopted on private sector–funded tunnels and tollways, these charges are based on investment returns and not on changing the behaviour of users across the network. Whereas reforms in other networked infrastructure sectors removed the model of effectively taxing businesses to cross-subsidise households, road funding models—by relying on indirect taxes that do not relate to the volume of usage—tend to cross-subsidise heavy users through light or even non-users of roads. Effectively, this leads to cross-subsidisation of road infrastructure and impacts on the supposedly competitive rail sector—hence the Australasian Railway Association's (2010: 21) support for the introduction of road pricing to ensure a level playing field between land transport modes. Further, where prices do not reflect volume of use, economic inefficiencies may result from externalities such as higher safety risks and further congestion and, subsequently, further degradation of roads. Changing transport behaviours is an important solution to traffic congestion, but the current system provides few incentives for users to reduce their reliance on road travel.

The primary purpose of a road user direct payment system (which might include volume-of-use charges combined with variable congestion charging during peak periods in central business districts) is to change commuter behaviour while at the same time rationalising road provision to better align it with strategic productivity considerations. Improvements in productivity require reduced traffic congestion and more effective use of transport infrastructure investment funds to deliver strategically important infrastructure. Building more and more roads into the future is unsustainable, and other approaches—such as changing traditional work and school hours—are unlikely to be achievable in the short term. Private sector investment entities have indicated that there are funds available for significant public–private partnerships (PPPs), and unsolicited infrastructure proposals, such as Transurban's recent East–West Link bid, are becoming an accepted way for governments to exploit infrastructure development opportunities.

But road reform is not *just* about roads. Transport reform may also contribute to other policy objectives, such as increasing physical activity or reducing environmental impacts through bicycle riding, the use of smaller vehicles (such as mopeds) or increased use of public transport. However, commuters are unlikely to change their behaviour under the current regime because existing road user charges are more akin to blunt access taxes, where, once paid, a consumer can exploit the provision to their heart's content. The charges convey negligible signals to road users about the costs of using particular roads, or to infrastructure providers about the demand for different roads. Furthermore, while investment in mass transit systems is under way—such as the Sydney and Melbourne metro systems, with major services opening in 2024—these systems will offer an alternative, large-scale option for commuters in Sydney and Melbourne. Introducing user charging to coincide with the availability of mass transit systems provides an ideal time to reform the planning, provision and maintenance of the road network, and incentivising behavioural changes that will help to decrease traffic congestion.

Previously, governments were prepared to tackle entrenched political obstacles to reform in introducing user-pays systems in public utilities and telecommunications services, but technological limitations, combined with entrenched interests, prevented reform of road pricing and provision. However, despite Professor Ian Harper's 2014 review of productivity acknowledging that technology is no longer an impediment to the implementation of a road user-pays system, and most transport-related interest groups calling for a road pricing and hypothecated funding system, there has been remarkably little policy action to date (Harper et al. 2015). Indeed, increased road provision has recently become a major federal election policy platform, utilising the existing funding model. As a result, the policy problem has become much more than how to adopt a particular pricing regime that will cover construction costs while encouraging more efficient use of transport infrastructure. Indeed, numerous technological and institutional mechanisms are well advanced overseas, already in implementation and have proven capability in delivering transport infrastructure efficiencies. The policy problem in Australia—like many other policy problems—relates to the impetus for reform and lack of political prioritisation. For instance, within the transport industry more generally, there is broad support for road charging reform on a user-pays basis. Yet, when economic or political opinion leaders—as opposed to industry advocates—meet, transport reform tends to be relegated to the 'too-hard basket' and supplanted by seemingly more pressing macroeconomic issues. Some commentators may argue that a focus on economic restructuring remains a pressing priority, but this places the transport industry in a difficult position: reform is easily achievable technically, yet incredibly difficult to implement without the necessary political will or the incentives for commuters to accept reform. It is clear that transport reform cannot be achieved by the transport industry working in isolation; a consolidated reform effort is required.

This book addresses two major questions that need to be answered if reform of the road pricing and provision system is to stimulate policy debate outside the industry:

- How can the terms of the public debate concerning infrastructure planning, provision and pricing be 'shifted' to address the long-term problems that will be brought about by not acting?
- How can commuters and road users be encouraged to develop a better understanding of longer-term issues of choice, pricing and interoperability of transport infrastructure?

This book highlights the major challenges to reform by bringing together some of the latest thinking on road pricing and provision in Australia, along with case studies from Singapore and New Zealand. The book addresses issues relating to three major transport infrastructure policy themes developed in consultation with the Australian Department of Infrastructure and Regional Development: 1) finding ways to better align the long-term planning of transport infrastructure with usage and productivity imperatives; 2) tackling the array of political and attitudinal impediments to achieving better infrastructure pricing and user-pays modes of pricing; and 3) translating technical capabilities and economic pricing theories into practice. While the book is intended to inform and stimulate discussion about future directions for transport infrastructure policy, and argue for a more sustainable and systemic mode of cost recovery, it does not attempt to advocate a single preferred solution to the current policy problems. Indeed, specific (or even optimal) policy solutions designed to address traffic congestion or improve freight movement are often mired in conflict with existing political realities. Infrastructure planning is frequently overshadowed by other concerns, such as private property rights, privacy rights and entrenched interests that make it all but impossible for governments to put the broader public interest forcibly ahead of narrow self-interest. Nonetheless, as Australia's major metropolitan centres continue to grow and—as we will demonstrate later—fuel excise revenues continue to decline, better integrated planning and some form of co-contribution charging will become increasingly important to ensure Australia's continued productivity and a better quality of life for citizens and commuters. The Harper (Harper et al. 2015) and Henry (Henry et al. 2010) reviews acknowledged that road reforms are among the most difficult to implement and will need to be conducted as part of a broader tax reform package. This book aims to provide a platform for elevating transport reform beyond the bounds of the transport industry—an important first step if road pricing and provision are to become key parts of the current reform agenda.

The book is divided into four sections. In Chapter 2, I consider where we are now and how we got here in developing a system of pricing and provision of road infrastructure. It has been noted that road reform cannot be done in isolation, and we find the story of roads was intertwined with rail and coastal shipping from the earliest days. In Section 2, we look to the long-term planning aspects of transport infrastructure. Marion Terrill considers the ways to reframe transport planning in Australia by shifting the debate away from an investment-only focus on big projects to considering transport as a complex social system interconnected with many spheres of policy. Philip Davies discusses Infrastructure Australia's strategic role in infrastructure planning, the importance of long-term and intermodal planning and preparing for population growth in our major metropolitan areas. Expertise contributed by Teik Soon Looi provides a case study of Singapore's world-class transport management network, outlining the challenges in reducing reliance on private vehicles and trialling new technologies in user charging, introducing advanced big data analysis for demand management and, soon, autonomous vehicles. Singapore's example in using market signals and incentives and disincentives to radically change transport behaviours provides interesting food for thought. Singapore is one of the few Asian capital cities (along with Tokyo) where transport mobility is effortless and congestion has been almost eliminated; the quality of life and movement in these planned transport cities compares outstandingly with other regional centres such as Jakarta, Beijing or Bangkok.

In Section 3, we look to how transport differs from other network technologies and at recent work on assessing the various options for road pricing and funding reform options. Alex Robson provides an economist's perspective on the difficulties governments will face in trying to convince motorists that reform is a good idea. He highlights how recent experience demonstrates how forecasts are rarely accurate and how a rigorous cost–benefit analysis can help in reducing policy errors. Brendon Lyon argues for a detailed public inquiry into road pricing and outlines the user-based approach adopted by Infrastructure Partnerships Australia in assessing the various options for road pricing. Interestingly, since the release of Infrastructure Australia's 15-year plan (see Chapter 4), the Turnbull Government has announced that an 'eminent Australian' will be chosen to lead a study into the costs and benefits of road pricing in the near future. Peter Winder concludes this section with a case study of Auckland's recent attempt to address shortcomings in infrastructure funding. He argues for the necessity and value of making political trade-offs explicit and transparent, and ensuring all stakeholders clearly understand both the trade-offs and associated constraints in initiating reform.

In the final section, we consider how to turn theory into practice. Professor Gary Banks draws on his long experience as the head of the Productivity Commission to detail the practical problems of addressing the concerns of the winners and losers of reform processes. The National Competition Policy reforms often faced stiff opposition, but strong technical and advisory support within key departments and political offices, and the importance of 'policy champions', are among the many practical lessons from these past successes. He argues that the need for change must become part of the policy narrative and it is up to political leaders to make a well-argued case that reform will make life better for Australian citizens. John Wanna concludes with an assessment of the prospects for and feasibility of reform pathways proposed by a selection of the more influential recent reports. His assessment considers the opportunities and challenges entailed when weighing up the various reform options and, in particular, highlights the implications for federal–state relations.

This monograph seeks to advance the road reform agenda by presenting some of the latest thinking on road pricing and provision from a variety of disciplinary approaches. It stresses the need for reform to ensure Australians can enjoy the benefits of efficient and sustainable transport infrastructure as our population and major cities continue to grow. Traffic congestion is avoidable, but we must act soon. The chapters presented here all point to the need for change; the expertise and the technology are available, and the various reform options have been mapped out in some detail. It is time for the policy debate to shift to how—rather than whether—road reform should progress.

References

Australasian Railway Association. (2010). *Road Pricing Reforms in Australia: Why Road Pricing is Vital to Australia's Economic Prosperity*. Canberra: Australasian Railway Association.

Bureau of Infrastructure, Transport and Regional Economics (BITRE). (2015). *Traffic and Congestion Cost Trends for Australian Capital Cities*. Information Sheet 74, November. Canberra: Commonwealth of Australia.

Bureau of Infrastructure, Transport and Regional Economics (BITRE). (2016). *Yearbook 2016: Australian Infrastructure Statistics*. Statistical Report. Canberra: Commonwealth of Australia.

Harper, I., Anderson, P., McCluskey, S. and O'Bryan, M. (2015). *Competition Policy Review: Final Report March 2015*. Canberra: Commonwealth of Australia. Available from: competitionpolicyreview.gov.au/files/2015/03/Competition-policy-review-report_online.pdf (accessed 12 August 2017).

Henry, K., Harmer, J., Piggott, J., Ridout, H. and Smith, G. (2010). *Australia's Future Tax System: Report to the Treasurer, Detailed Analysis Volume 2*. Canberra: Commonwealth of Australia.

2

Road pricing and road provision in Australia: Where are we and how did we get here?

Michael de Percy

In the beginning

British settlement of Australia began in 1788 and, from the outset, governments of all persuasions imposed strong 'statist' traditions of public ownership and control of important infrastructure. Economic development and physical access across the continent were dependent on statist investment, construction and maintenance of crucial infrastructure—often called the 'colonial liberalist' legacy by subsequent historians. State intervention was accepted as a basic requirement of social progress and economic development and, over time, Australia became locked in a 'path dependency' paradigm reliant on state provision and regulation of vital infrastructure. Accordingly, the provision of modes of transport across the continent and the policy dictates associated with the crucial issues of provision and usage were framed within a particularly statist mindset. Roads, rail, shipping and river transport, as well as bridges, jetties and wharves (and later air transport), were all historically financed and governed by *dirigisme* and by institutional arrangements, rather than market-based measures such as private investment, private provision and consumer charging.[1] Arguably, command-driven public provision and the arbitrary governmental regulation of transport infrastructure came at a cost to the overall productivity and efficiency of each type of infrastructure and the interconnectivity between them. And we are still living with the legacy of this pattern of state activism in the funding and provision of transport infrastructure.

The development of the railways across Australia is a good example. Colonies, and later states, invested heavily in extensive rail networks, opening up land and forests, connecting farms and towns and servicing urban areas. Rail was more important than roads. States funded these networks with capital borrowed from British banks, thereby generating enormous state debts at the subnational level. While the Commonwealth gradually had to assist in repaying these debts, the states guarded their individual rail systems with monopolistic regulations imposed on usage (and, to some extent, by formulating non-standard specifications such as different rail gauges—an early form of regulatory protection). *Rail preferencing*, especially for the movement of freight, was a feature of Australian development for almost a century. As Hancock (1930: 55) argued during this period, Australia '[h]as come to look upon the State as a vast public utility, whose duty is to provide the greatest happiness for the greatest number'.

He continued (Hancock 1930: 110, 112–13), using the vast state railways as an example:

> Let us consider the railways, for upon them rests the economic structure of each one of the States. In 1927–28 nearly one-half of the existing public debt of the States had been incurred on their behalf. In that year the deficits to which all the Australian railways confessed amounted to about £5,500,000. Yet in the three years prior to the war the railways had (at least in appearance) paid their way; they had even contributed to the various treasuries an aid of about £800,000. The difficulties of railways in post-war years, and particularly the difficulty of competing with road transport, are notorious all the world over … So, then the railways become an instrument for subsidizing 'development', for promoting decentralization for protecting local industry, for cherishing Naboth, for inaugurating the new social order. But this is confusion. The railways are not really an effective instrument for these assorted purposes. All these

---

1   There were a few isolated examples of private provision of infrastructure—such as bridges and toll roads—but these were usually gradually incorporated into state-provided systems (see Sturgess 1996).

miscellaneous demands upon their good nature make it more difficult for them to fulfil their own essential purpose, which is to provide adequate transport for goods and passengers at the lowest possible cost.

Hence, rail transport dominated the movement of freight and passengers until a 1954 decision by the Privy Council in London ended the protection of state government–owned railways (The Age 1954: 3). This decision to break the rail monopoly was historically significant in that, once these institutional barriers were removed, the majority share of the volume of freight moved by land transport shifted from rail to road. Coastal shipping—which was to some extent in competition with rail—had steadily declined and effectively disappeared from the transport policy narrative by this time (Fitchett 1976: 7). Indeed, only very recently have the institutional arrangements for coastal shipping been identified as barriers to increasing its share of bulk freight transport (Standing Committee on Infrastructure, Transport, Regional Development and Local Government and King 2008).

The legacy of the regulatory arrangements regarding rail freight, shipping and road haulage did not encourage active competition to increase efficiencies and contain costs between the different transport modes, or lead to better integration and interoperability. Indeed, the reverse occurred. When the highly regulated institutional arrangements that governed the state-owned and operated rail networks (which also allowed them to recover their costs) were eventually dismantled, the state rail systems soon became poorly performing commercial ventures, unable to pay their way, and experienced a long-term historical decline accompanied by the wholesale closure of branch-line rail networks. By contrast, road freight transport had been captured by private hauliers and transport firms who, along with passenger transporters and private motorists, all viewed roads and the road systems as free 'public goods', provided from general taxation by governments to connect regions and communities. Such thinking meant that while governments were pressured to invest in new roads and development road projects, they did not raise sufficient funds from road users to fund road building or to reflect the costs of road maintenance. In other words, while governments were forced to expand their road networks, it was difficult for them to efficiently charge road users for the full costs of provision and capture negative externalities such as the cost of maintenance. This discrepancy created subsequent problems for intermodal competition in that the cost of road transport was heavily subsidised, whereas rail was meant to be operated on a cost-recovery basis, even though many rail lines, in fact, lost money. Moreover, governments found that they were expected to replicate the existing rail corridors and connections, which, arguably, led to the misallocation of investment dollars.

A second legacy of the earlier dominance of rail monopolies resulted in a general decline in road provision and maintenance (BTE 1977: 387). With the changed regulatory environment after the 1950s, and as freight and passenger movement became more reliant on the road network, state governments with relatively small tax bases struggled to fund improvements to their road systems. This gradually led to a greater role for the Commonwealth to fund national highways through the annual tied grants programs. Increased specific commitments by the Commonwealth for the funding of major road infrastructure improvements have been a feature of federal–state relations since the 1960s. However, despite the Commonwealth's involvement and the increasing importance of the road network, and the extent of the National Competition Policy reforms of the 1980s, Australia's road infrastructure remains the 'least reformed of all infrastructure sectors, with institutional arrangements around funding and provision remaining much the same as they were 20 years ago' (Harper et al. 2015: 28–30).

Regulatory reform in the road transport sector has focused mainly on issues of road safety, vehicle inspection and heavy vehicle regulation. As the quantity and capacity of heavy road vehicles increased, governmental attention to road usage increased exponentially—directed mainly towards the levels of investment in and maintenance of roads, and often related to safety measures. By the 2010s, while rail still dominated bulk freight transportation (carrying cargo such as coal, iron ore and grain; see Figure 2.1), road haulage dominated the non-bulk freight task (Figure 2.2). This pattern has been manifested since deregulation of road transport took effect in the early 1970s (BTE 1977). In recent decades, the propensity of rail to carry bulk freight and for non-bulk freight to go by road has increased sharply. By contrast, coastal shipping tonnages have remained largely stable, although the sector's share of the freight task has declined in relation to road and rail. The 2008 Coastal Shipping Inquiry conducted by the Australian Parliament acknowledged that this declining share in the freight task means more freight on road and rail services, which are already under pressure.

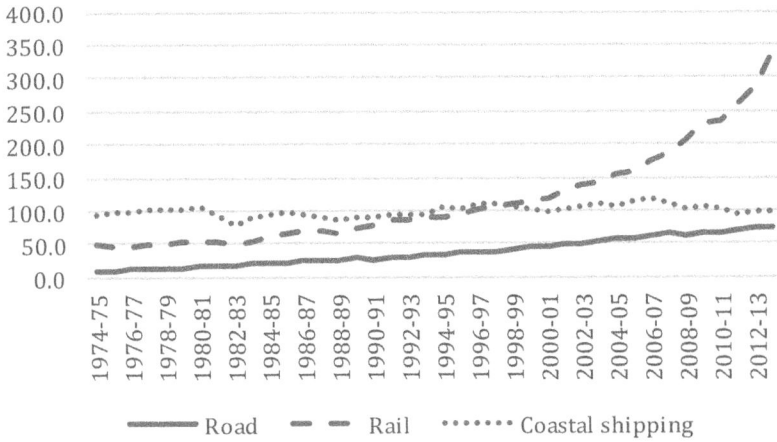

Figure 2.1 Bulk freight task by mode (billion tonne kilometres)
Source: BITRE (2016: Table T 2.1a).

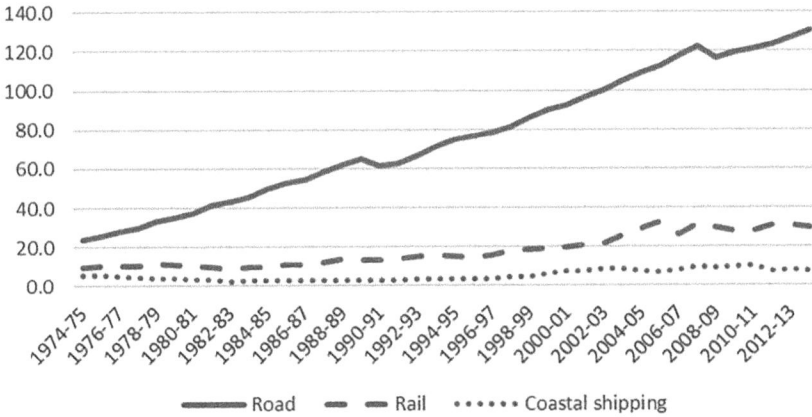

Figure 2.2 Non-bulk freight task by mode (billion tonne kilometres)
Source: BITRE (2016: Table T 2.1b).

The complex relationship between road and rail transport in Australia not only has a long history, but also has many dimensions and paradoxes. As railways were deployed, there was a tendency for roads to be left to decline or remain unsealed. Until the 1954 Privy Council decision, rail passenger travel was heavily cross-subsidised by requirements that all freight of a certain size and moving over a certain distance had to travel by rail. As a result, state railways tended to operate at a surplus. Only after the Privy Council decision enabled competition from road transport did the state railways begin to run at a loss. So, over time, the waxing and waning of the road and rail transport industries were largely due not to the commercial disciplines of the market, but to the consequences of policy decisions and the regulatory framework. The pattern of 'trading off' between road and rail modes may have occurred out of economic necessity and, for the most part, the supply of passenger and freight transport options in the past was at least adequate to meet the demands of population growth and the level of economic activity. In the present, however, the current supply of both road and rail transport infrastructure in Australia is nowhere near meeting demand. Furthermore, projections into the next 30 years suggest the consequences of inadequate investment in transport infrastructure, coupled with the inefficient transport behaviour of users, will lead to significant costs and a potential lowering of the standard of living. Nevertheless, ways of dealing with these issues have been proposed for some time.

Changing paradigms: Pricing, planning and behaviour

Celebrated economists and urban planners such as Arthur Pigou (pricing) and Le Corbusier (planning) identified issues affecting the pricing and planning of road networks as early as the 1920s. Pigou (1920) proposed a tax to equal negative externalities, and his ideas were taken up by William Vickrey (1948: 227; 1963: 457), who saw them as a means to introduce congestion charging to influence the behaviour of road users and investors. In planning, Le Corbusier (1987) examined the long-term impact of historical legacies on the roads of Paris from the Middle Ages, which were based on the easiest routes for pack animals to negotiate. He considered this pattern obsolete and contemplated the complete replacement of existing thoroughfares to make them more suited for automobiles. For Le Corbusier, the complete redesign and rebuilding of road systems was required, rather than tinkering with existing networks, which would not solve the basic problems.

Australian governments have, over time, acknowledged these two major issues of pricing and planning. However, the challenges of recalibrating the entire system of transportation have proved to be politically difficult. The task would have involved two aspects. First, governments would have had to undo the legacy of an (inadequate) cost-recovery funding system that has been collected predominantly through general taxes and flat levies, with no obvious correlation between road use and taxes paid. Second, and following that, governments would have to overcome the legacies of past transport infrastructure planning and design, where rail routes, for example, were based on the capacity of steam locomotives, ventured to remote parts of the states and connected long-exhausted remote mining ventures or small rural towns. In more recent times, these routes did not efficiently connect the major country towns, nor were they optimal to provide services to travellers.

In Australia, road and rail transport infrastructure has remained largely under government ownership and control, and therefore negative externalities have been captured through taxation more generally (and often via policies focused on specific issues such as transport safety, noise, environmental pollution and urban renewal). Further, state governments have adopted a variety of planning responses, ranging from the organic (Sydney, Brisbane) to the planned (Melbourne, Adelaide, Perth). There is some irony, however, in the different outcomes of the two approaches. For example, Sydney addressed the traffic congestion problem created by rail level crossings early in its history, partly because of geography, but also because of the sprawling nature of the city and its traffic routes. Melbourne, on the other hand, with its light rail network and orderly road system, did not focus on the removal of level crossings until an allocation in the 2015–16 budget, with the removal of some 50 level crossings required to improve safety and congestion, to be conducted over eight years. Further, Melbourne has only recently addressed the legacies of the light rail network's outdated congestion-causing rail tracks crisscrossing the centre of the city. The combination of pricing and planning legacies has led to numerous responses from government, but usually pricing emerges as a way to fund critical new infrastructure that may or may not have been in the 'pipeline' of major infrastructure projects.

The challenges created by historical legacies are numerous and relate to issues ranging from planning approval (such as 'corridor preservation') to behaviours around the use of the infrastructure (such as an expectation that roads are public goods and therefore their use should be free to all). Road user charges, or tolls, have been used sparingly by Australian governments to recover the costs of investment—in particular, for infrastructure projects such as the Sydney Harbour Bridge and Brisbane's Gateway Bridge and for a web of tunnels carrying freeway traffic under city centres, rivers and harbours. While improved engineering methods allowed the Hume Highway to be rerouted to bypass smaller towns and to make road travel between Sydney and Melbourne faster and safer, many of the existing rail lines in New South Wales (NSW), Victoria and South Australia still follow routes designed around the limitations of steam-driven engines to connect farming communities. While there are now more private toll roads and private railways in Australia, road and rail infrastructure generally remains under government control, with the Commonwealth assuming an increasing political role for the allocation of road funding. In recent years, the Commonwealth has sought to claim some 'dividend' from its partial asset ownership in such projects, but states and territories have been reluctant to engage with them on this matter; the Commonwealth could impose its preferences by insisting payments of dividends from recipient states become a condition of specific-purpose payment funding (and most likely the states would be reluctantly forced to accede).

Throughout the various states and territories, existing road user charges are based on a 'two-part tariff' model, where road users pay a flat 'network access charge' (state-based motor vehicle registration fees tied to vehicle size and/or location) and a quasi user charge based on fuel consumption (the Commonwealth's fuel excise on petrol, diesel and liquid petroleum gas, or LPG). However, there is no obvious link between these charges and investment in and maintenance of roads. Nor is there a close link between these fees and levies and actual patterns of usage or usage in times of high congestion. For instance, a driver travelling 10,000 km in Sydney's central business district (CBD) would pay exactly the same fuel excise as a driver covering the same distances on virtually unused country roads. Increasingly, fuel efficiency has also reduced the amount of revenue raised through the fuel excise, with those owning older cars tending to pay more for their use of the roads than those driving more efficient vehicles. While heavy vehicles pay higher fees for road use and access, there is no direct link between the damage done by these vehicles and the resulting cost of maintenance.

When the goods and services tax (GST) was introduced in 2000, the indexation of fuel excise was temporarily discontinued. Despite the fuel excise being increased biannually in line with the consumer price index (CPI) since 2014, revenue from fuel excise continues to decline and local governments—responsible for the majority of roads—still struggle to find adequate funds to maintain existing roads. Meanwhile, the Commonwealth—which has no direct constitutional responsibility for roads, and in fact owns or controls very few roads on the continent—has taken on a greater role in funding roads through successive federal governments using road funding as a major policy platform for electioneering purposes. The result has been to increase the availability and capacity of roads, without an increase in funding to maintain either existing or new roads.

Australia has reached the point where, in the future, the consequences of 'doing nothing' will inevitably lead to increasing costs. This will be due to massive traffic congestion in the major cities, fuelled by population growth, rising affluence and unchecked demand. Moreover, there will be a decreased capacity for freight and passenger movement on the road network due to a lack of upgrading and maintenance. When combined with the lack of investment in alternative transport modes—particularly high-speed rail—there are few incentives for motorists or truck operators to change their behaviour and reduce demand on the existing road infrastructure. Evidence from overseas jurisdictions, such as California, clearly indicates that states cannot build their way out of traffic congestion; they merely add to it exponentially. Indeed, increasing the capacity of roads simply increases the demand for them, and reinforces existing road use behaviours. It creates perverse logics and outcomes.

Following this argument, it is apparent that two things need to occur on the policy front. First, there needs to be an increase in investment in alternative transport modes, particularly rail, which can move freight and greater numbers of people efficiently and speedily. Second, there needs to be a way to modify the current behaviour of road users to encourage efficient use of existing roads. Planning and pricing, then, are the keys to improving the efficiency of passenger and freight transport in Australia. The problems, of course, are first, how to prioritise and fund infrastructure projects and, second, and much more importantly, how to garner political support for an appropriate road pricing system so that the patterns of usage change to facilitate network efficiencies and maximise user satisfaction.

At the heart of the public policy problem is the entrenched perception of roads as a free public good for which users do not need to pay (despite roads not being wholly a 'public good' in definitional terms; one person's enjoyment of the good can impact on another's enjoyment through congestion). Users see roads and their usage of them more or less as an inalienable 'right', and itemised payments for the use of roads through tolls and charges as an annoying infringement of these same rights. Road tolls of even miniscule levels irritate passenger vehicle drivers beyond belief, and where specific toll-based infrastructure is built to alleviate congestion it is not clear that truck drivers or tradespeople who have to pay the toll personally (not their firms) will take the optimal option. Part of the problem is that road users do not experience the charges they are already paying for road access and use as that use actually occurs. Tolls, however, provide a point-of-sale signal, whether a beep on the dashboard or an online credit card payment, which clearly links usage with the price.

This problem is further exacerbated by the lack of a direct link between road user charges and investment in transport infrastructure and maintenance. The current two-part tariff does not provide users (or, indeed, investors) with price signals that can effectively modify behaviour. This occurs because there is no information provided to the consumer at the point of sale that directly correlates with their use of the infrastructure (DIRD 2016: 41). In comparison, consumers of energy, water and telecommunications services will modify their behaviours in the use of these services because there is a clear price signal at the point of sale, and they incur an itemised bill. Hence, the more consumers use the services, the more they pay; therefore, patterns of usage are necessarily constrained by the consumer's budget and their motivation to save money. Road usage is not so rationed or priced to change unnecessary usage or usage in peak congestion periods. We pay the price of congested usage indirectly in *time* by waiting in queues and enduring endless traffic jams, but we do not count the collective cost of these wasted hours, fuel, mental frustration and opportunities in terms of what other useful things those trapped in the endless tailgates could undertake.

While paying excise taxes for fuel does represent a quasi user charge, as the number of fuel-efficient vehicles increases, these price signals are decreasing accordingly. Yet, road users continue to use roads without paying directly for the proportionate use of them (or the congestion they cause) and, as the revenue from the fuel excise declines, governments increasingly pick up the tab for the supply and maintenance of road infrastructure, despite increasing demand by road users. This means that low-volume users of roads, and those with less fuel-efficient vehicles, are cross-subsidising high-volume users. It also means that the true cost of road freight is not being captured in the price of freighted goods. Consumers still pay the price for these externalities through increased taxes and other opaque input charges, but the price is not visible to the consumer, nor does it factor to change their behaviour.

With general levies and charges there are no clear signals for the demand for transport infrastructure beyond the collective voice of road users in their dissatisfaction with traffic congestion or poorly maintained roads. The same principle applies to road freight. Rather than improving rail freight services, policy thinking is dominated by road freight to such an extent that addressing shortfalls in the non-bulk freight task has led to calls to increase the capacity of freight trucks—from B-double to B-triple. Such thinking sees consideration of the externalities relating to road safety, increased maintenance costs due to rampant damage of road surfaces and increased congestion on major freight routes relegated to the achievement of the freight carrying task. It is interesting that road freight, using vehicles with ever-increasing capacities, is being considered on the Hume Highway (connecting Sydney and Melbourne) when there is an existing viable railway line between the two major cities. Given that a freight train can move maybe 1,000 times more than a single B-triple truck and, additionally, the rail network suffers less from use than the road network, it is arguable that externalities relating to road network use are not being captured appropriately in the price of road freight.

Not surprisingly, then, rail industry advocates have been major supporters of road pricing reform, with a rail inquiry and numerous reports by the Australasian Railway Association recommending road pricing as a means to improve intermodal competition. It is interesting that the rail industry is now in a similar position to that of the road transport industry before the 1954 Privy Council decision. Then, competition between rail and road was prevented by legislation. Now, competition between rail and road is reduced by the subsidisation of road transport inherent in the two-part tariff system and the funding of road infrastructure through unrelated revenue streams. Rail transport tends to be more expensive as the price of rail travel reflects more of the costs of inputs and usage than the price of road travel. It may be said, then, that the existing system encourages freight behaviours based on inadequate pricing signals. Rather than encourage improvements in rail infrastructure, perceptions of cheaper prices associated with road freight, particularly at the point of sale, encourage increased capacity in the existing system, leading to the problems discussed above.

Similar behaviours can be observed among business investors weighing up potentially profitable infrastructural investments, despite increased interest from superannuation and private equity funds in investing in infrastructure (Anthony 2016; Desloires 2016). The preponderance of infrastructure 'announcements' by various Australian governments for electioneering purposes (pork-barrelling), coupled with established attitudes and behaviours towards road usage, has tended to restrict the private sector's role in building infrastructure to public–private partnerships (PPPs) with government. While this is not necessarily a bad thing, it means that transport infrastructure is captured by political processes rather than by clear economic principles. Conversely, it may be said that there is more to life than economic efficiency, but given the economic consequences of the status quo are forecast to reduce Australia's living standards and, indeed, our quality of life, it is important that the way we conduct planning, provision and use of transport infrastructure leads to increases in economic efficiency. There is much literature to support the need for Australia to do so (see, for example, BITRE 2014; DIRD 2014, 2016; Harper et al. 2015; Henry et al. 2010; Juturna Consulting 2012; Laird 2014; OECD 2010, 2012, 2014, 2017), and motorists in any of Australia's major metropolitan centres are surely aware of the extent of the existing problems with traffic congestion. But whether those same motorists (and also governments) are prepared to change their behaviours to enable the required efficiencies to occur is quite another matter. And, for as long as road funding and provision remain a political rather than an economic issue, without strong leadership, transport reform is unlikely to occur.

Revenue, expenditure and changing perceptions

The reaction of the Australian public to talk of road user charges has typically remained negative. And the tabloid press has milked the outrage for all it is worth. For example, after colluding with the *Sunday Telegraph* about the issue of road user charging (O'Rourke 2015), the *Daily Telegraph* tested a mooted charge of 1.5 cents per kilometre (based on a similar voluntary scheme in Oregon) or a $10 congestion charge (which would appear to be based on the London zonal congestion charges) and put these propositions to Sydney residents (O'Rourke 2015). Predictably, there was community outrage. One respondent—a locksmith who travelled 70 km a day for his business—preferred things to stay as they were. He believed it was 'not fair if we end up having to pay more to do our jobs just because someone wants to get more cars off the road'. To have to pay for the use of the road—which, to him, was a necessity for his business—even if a fuel rebate was applied, would see him 'out of pocket'. Further, the *Sunday Telegraph*'s editorial challenged the fairness of paying a user charge on a road system that was effectively a daily car park, especially when there was no other modal choice available for many users and commuters (Saleh 2015). For users to be asked to pay a charge for use of a road that they seem to have no choice other than to use can be seen as little more than revenue raising, rather than a means of changing behaviours and providing market information. For policymakers, such negative views of road pricing will not be easy to overcome—much like voters' aversion to a value-added or GST consumption tax during the late stages of the twentieth century.

The implementation of the GST (see Chapter 7, this volume) provides an interesting counterfactual to the potential doom surrounding road pricing and, indeed, lessons about how road pricing can be introduced. After years of political debate over the introduction of a consumption tax, it was only through the leadership of John Howard and Peter Costello that the GST came to be. Former Liberal opposition leader John Hewson's infamous GST 'birthday cake' demonstrated the political problem of trying to explain something seemingly simple but technically very complex. Nevertheless, once introduced and despite the political trade-offs with Democrats' leader Meg Lees resulting in a rather narrow conception of the proposed broad-based consumption tax, the GST has not resulted in the doom and gloom predicted before its introduction. Yet the GST was a major reform that, accompanied with lower income taxes, has been generally positive in its impact on individuals and businesses. That is not to say the GST does not require further reform, but the biggest sticking point today with road funding (see Chapter 10) is how we reform the broken system where revenues historically viewed as the purview of the states and collected by state treasuries will be collected and redistributed by the Commonwealth.

Nonetheless, behavioural change by road users will be key to reducing congestion and improving the efficiency of Australia's transport infrastructure. Road and rail infrastructure spending has increased as a percentage of gross domestic product (GDP) in the past decade and grew from 0.69 per cent in 1986–87 to 1.23 per cent in 2015–16 (Figure 2.3). Clearly, the problem is not principally a lack of infrastructure spending, but a case of using the existing infrastructure more efficiently. Moreover, road-related revenue and expenditure have been steadily increasing on all fronts and at all levels of government. The details of each part of the revenue and expenditure regime are worth briefly noting.

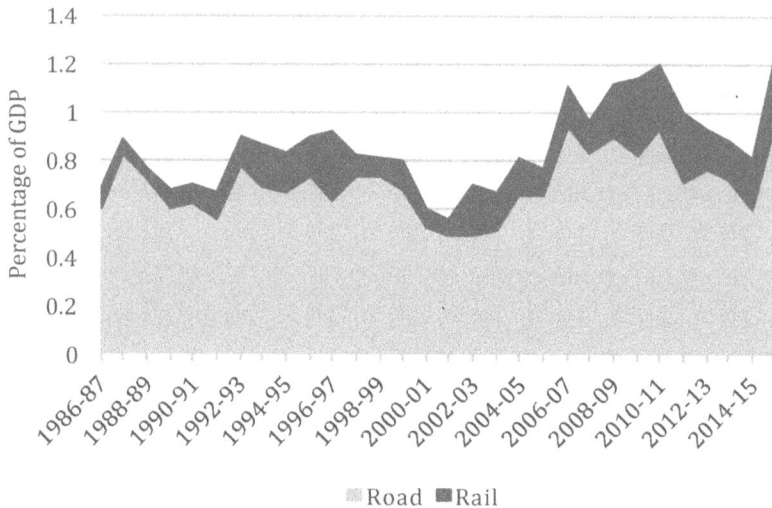

Figure 2.3 Road and rail infrastructure expenditure as a percentage of gross domestic product (GDP)
Sources: ABS (2017a: Table 3; 2017b: Table 11).

Total public sector road-related revenue has steadily risen in the past decade, allowing for the 2008 Global Financial Crisis (GFC) (Figure 2.4). However, the mix of revenue items has changed, with increases in state and territory revenues (Figure 2.5) the most significant growth area in public sector revenue increase (along with the GST on road-related consumption). Of these, the largest growth is evident in the proportion of vehicle registration fees and tolls. While increases in tolls reflect the use of relevant parts of the road network, the network access charge (vehicle registrations)—which tends to reinforce perceptions of roads as public goods—is increasing, providing motorists with a 'double-whammy' effect: increased access fees and charges for sitting gridlocked in traffic. Meanwhile, the fuel excise, which represents a quasi user charge, is declining steadily (Figure 2.6). Road-related expenditure is also increasing across the public sector generally (Figure 2.7) and for the Commonwealth (Figure 2.8), state and territory (Figure 2.9) and local levels of government (Figure 2.10).

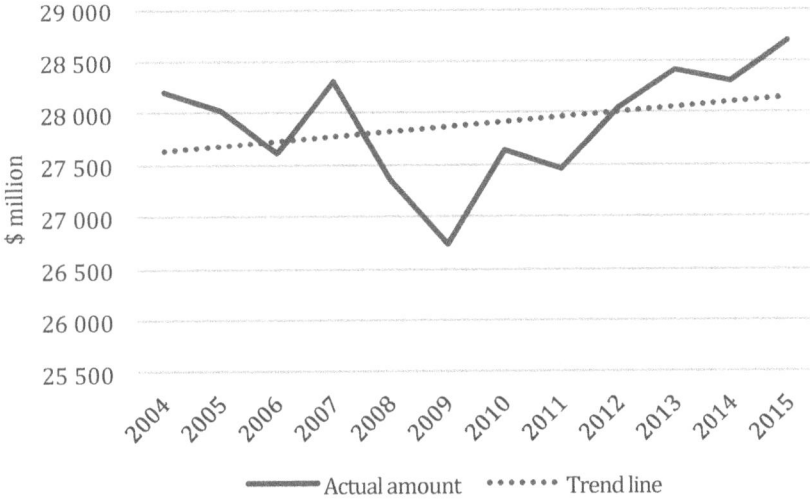

Figure 2.4 Total public sector road-related revenue in Australia (2015 prices)

Source: BITRE (2016).

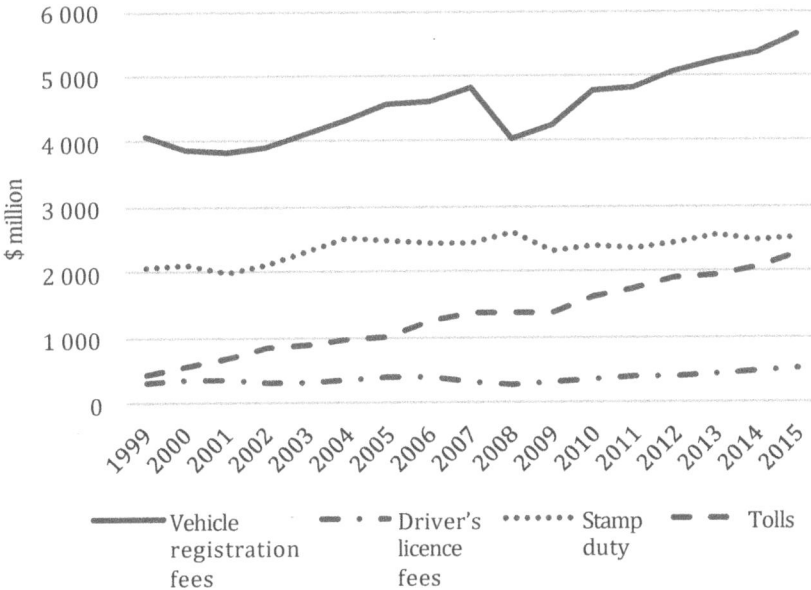

Figure 2.5 State and territory road-related revenue by type (2015 prices)

Source: BITRE (2016).

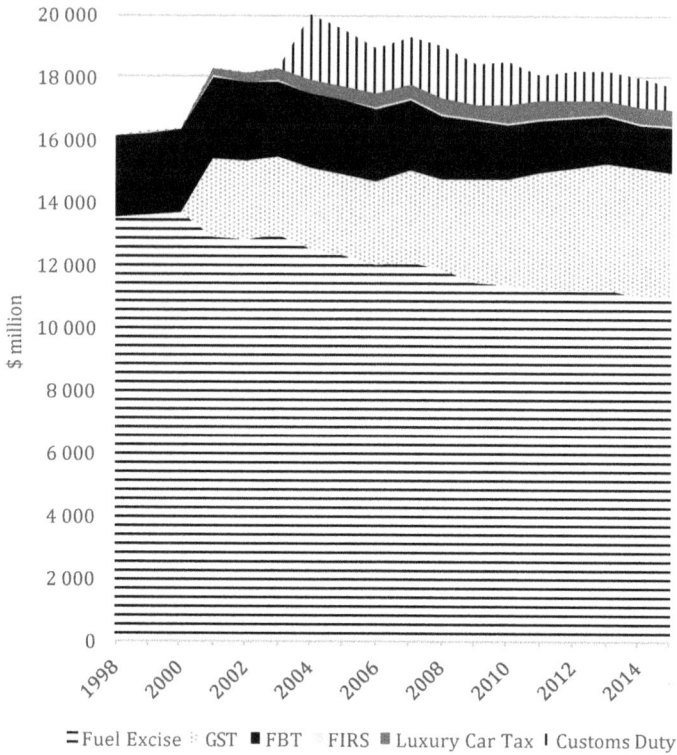

Figure 2.6 Commonwealth road-related revenue by type (2015 prices)
Source: BITRE (2016).

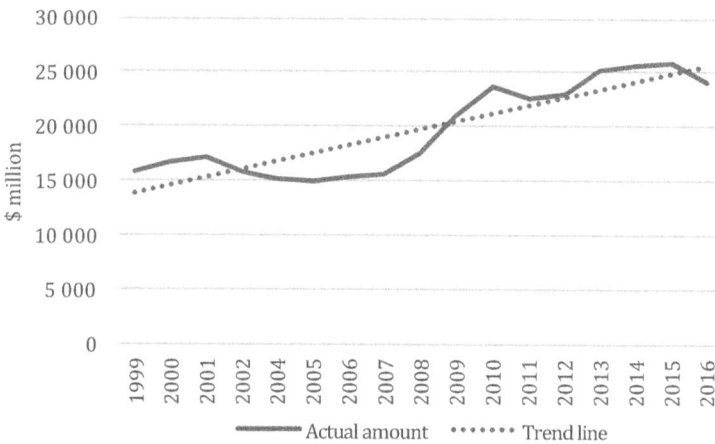

Figure 2.7 Total public sector road-related expenditure for Australia (2015 prices)
Source: BITRE (2016).

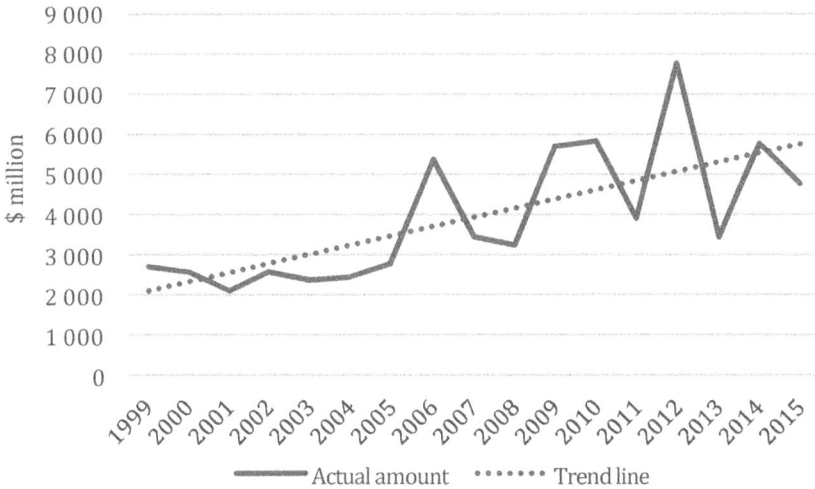

Figure 2.8 Total Commonwealth road-related expenditure (2015 prices)
Source: BITRE (2016).

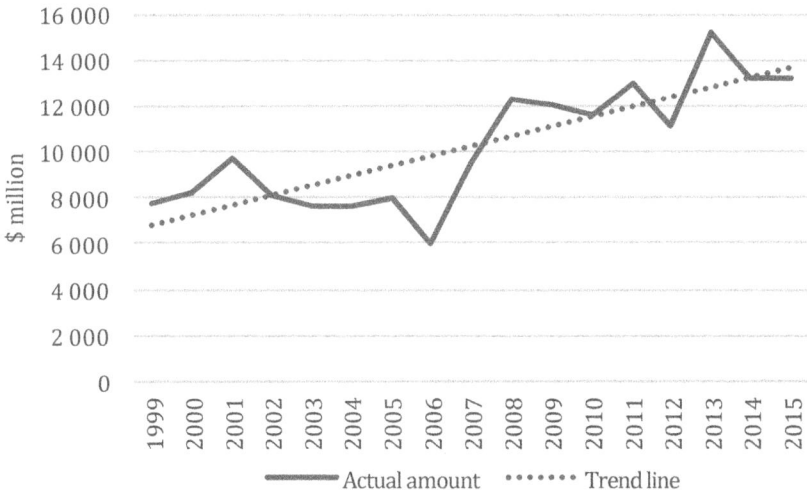

Figure 2.9 Total state and territory government road-related expenditure (2015 prices)
Source: BITRE (2016).

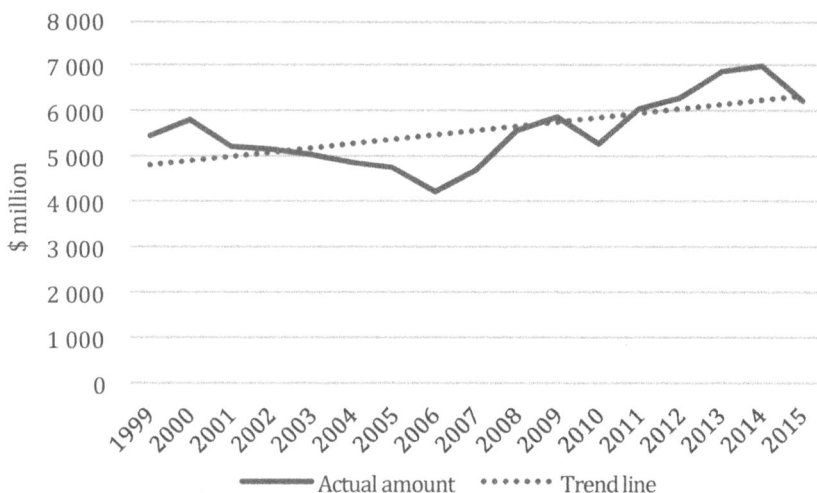

Figure 2.10 Total local government road-related expenditure (2015 prices)
Source: BITRE (2016).

In its examination of road-related revenue and expenditure trends, the Department of Infrastructure and Regional Development (DIRD 2016: 41) noted:

> While there is only very limited hypothecation of road-related revenue to road expenditure, the cost of building and maintaining our roads is increasing at a rate faster than road-related revenue collected from motorists in taxes and charges.
>
> Aspects of the current system of road-related fees and charges, such as fixed registration charges and stamp duty, do not provide a direct signal to road users about the cost of service provision and can encourage inefficient use of road services.
>
> Population growth, urban development and changes in the broader economy will increase future demand on road infrastructure and, based on current trends, congestion is forecast to increase in major urban areas, which will constrain productivity. Without improved congestion management, the net social costs of congestion are expected to almost double over the next 15 years. The avoidable social cost of congestion in the eight Australian capitals was estimated to be approximately $16.5 billion in the 2015 financial year [in 2010 dollars], rising from about $12.8 billion in 2010. These costs are projected to rise further to around $30 billion by 2030 without measures to cut congestion.

Clearly, the long-established mix of road-related revenue and expenditure is unsustainable into the future, and the idea of hypothecation is not new. Indeed, when it was introduced in 1929, the fuel excise was tied to road funding, and this was not changed to general revenue until 1959. Road-related revenue may not be tied to roads, but consumers expect it to be so. But consumers are not the only ones who are reluctant to see a change to how we pay for roads. Since 1959, successive federal governments have been reluctant to restrict their ability to raise general revenue and to tie policy expenditure to hypothecated revenue. There is some merit to this principle. In 1990, then minister for land transport in the Australian Labor Party Government, Bob Brown, explained:

[In] our seven years we have increased funding in a period of very tight fiscal restraint by 18 percent over and above the seven years of our predecessors. That represents, in terms of dollars, an additional $19.6 billion in today's terms, in today's prices that we've put into the road system. We shouldn't, any more than we say we'll determine how much we'll put into education on the basis of how much income tax school teachers pay. That would be absurd. It's equally absurd for us to say that we will determine our level of road funding on the basis of how much tax motorists pay … So we're not about y'know, that whole question of hypothecation, determining how much we'll put into roads on the basis of how much tax comes from any particular source. (Department of Prime Minister and Cabinet 1990)

An important change to note, however, is that, by 1990, the federal government had taken a lead role in funding roads, one that had been steadily increasing since the removal of protection from state rail services. The increasing demand for road freight transport led to the *Commonwealth Aid Roads Act 1959*, which ceased hypothecation of fuel excise and introduced a formula for allocating funds to states based on a combination of population, area and the number of registered vehicles with a quota of state funding to be provided to obtain the allocated federal funding (but out of consolidated revenue) (Clark 1988: 285). By 1969, the Commonwealth Bureau of Roads (CBR) had been established and increasingly sophisticated formulas were adopted to achieve efficiency measures in investment allocation in line with growing demand for roads. The CBR 'recommended the creation of a system of national highways' and, by 1974, 'program approval was required for state road expenditure to ensure that "national objectives [were] taken fully into account"' (Jones 1974: 382, cited in Clark 1988: 287). Constitutionally, the Commonwealth could not direct or enforce specific levels of state expenditure on roads. However, its various leveraging formulas enabled it to withhold funding from the states if national objectives were not being achieved through state expenditure. Hence, the Commonwealth was gradually able to 'impose its will' on the states (Clark 1988: 287).

While some state discretion was preserved during the Fraser Government's 'New Federalism' period, the Australian Bicentennial Road Development (ABRD) program adopted a hypothecated fuel tax (in addition to the fuel excise) from 1982 to 1988 to fund Commonwealth road projects through a form of specific-purpose grants. This enabled the Commonwealth to leverage control over policy areas of state responsibility, and was showcased by road signs advertising the Commonwealth's role in funding roads for the community. Since this period in particular, the constitutional powers over roads generally ascribed to the states have been in conflict with the Commonwealth's financial powers, and an accepted formula for funding roads remains a sore point with the states (Clark 1988: 287; Head et al. 1990; Holderhead 2017). Despite improved government marketing of road funding initiatives, and increased road funding being used for election purposes, the period from the late 1980s until the early 2000s witnessed generally flat growth in funding, with the Commonwealth providing the smallest share of the three tiers of government (Webb 2004: 16). Nevertheless, Commonwealth funding of roads has trended upward and road funding continues to play a politically important role, such as the Roads to Recovery program, which will provide some $4.4 billion from 2013–14 to 2020–21 'to Australia's local councils, state and territory Governments responsible for local roads' (DIRD 2017b). So, finding the right formula for reform will require a significant shift of the debate on road pricing and provision if the emerging institutional framework is to be sustainable.

Where we live, how we commute and ideas about equity

Urban sprawl has been a perennial feature of Australian cities, predicated on the widespread take-up of the motor car. The use of cars as a major mode of travel continued to grow from the 1920s until the mid-2000s, after which car use has generally levelled out or appeared to decline on a per capita basis. There has been much research into this observed phenomenon seeking to explain the reasons behind this historical 'peak' and then slightly declining trend. Three alternative hypotheses have been proposed—namely, 'peak car usage', 'saturation of use' and 'interrupted growth' (OECD and ITF 2013). Peak car usage is based on the idea that the number of kilometres travelled by privately owned cars has reached its finite peak, and the car as an essential means of individual transport is therefore on the decline. Reasons for the decline in motor vehicle usage include changes in attitudes towards living conditions and the preference of professionals, particularly the younger generation, to live in inner cities and commute via public transport, cycling and walking. Living in the inner city, the need for a car is decreased. Newman (2015) suggested that, by 2004, the peak in car usage had occurred in all major Australian cities, and therefore fears about increasing urban traffic congestion were unfounded (see Newman and Kenworthy 2011). Increased congestion was generally portrayed as a major policy challenge by authorities such as Infrastructure Australia (2015), in the *Australian Infrastructure Audit*, and BITRE (2015a), in the *State of Australian Cities 2014–2015* report. Newman suggested the observable travel behaviours of younger generations were changing and, accordingly, he proposed better planning for travel by modes such as cycling, walking and light rail. He argued that, as car travel on a per capita basis continued to decline, these alternative modes of transport would further decrease demand for urban car usage and thus alleviate congestion problems.

While it may be plausible that car usage has peaked on the basis of per capita kilometres travelled by car, this does not necessarily mean a reduction in traffic congestion on highly congested road systems. Indeed, the modelling by Infrastructure Australia (2015) and BITRE (2015b) has predicted the major driver of urban traffic congestion will be population growth rather than the number of kilometres travelled by individual drivers. Although car use has historically increased as incomes have risen, BITRE's (2015b: 5) projections adopt the 'saturation' hypothesis, in which car use as a proportion of population is expected to peak by 2020 because 'people are spending as much time on daily travel as they are willing to commit; and are loath to spend any more of their limited time budgets on yet more travel, even if incomes do happen to rise'.

Interrupted growth is a worst-case scenario. According to this hypothesis, car usage has slowed due to a combination of 'national incomes measured as GDP per head, population, and fuel cost of motoring' (Goodwin 2013: 78). However, based on what is assumed about future combinations of these factors, 'car traffic will continue to grow, albeit at a slowing rate, for several decades into the future' (OECD and ITF 2013: 78). The above three approaches to understanding car use are merely plausible hypotheses, and therefore inconclusive in determining future trends in individual car use. BITRE's approach is to adopt 'saturation' as the middle position, where road use will remain at present rates for the medium term, but congestion will remain an issue due to population growth (BITRE 2015b: 7). Such a conservative approach is warranted, given the emergence of self-driving or driverless cars.

Driverless cars present a major opportunity to reduce traffic congestion by automating driving actions and organising (or 'platooning') vehicles to allow for more efficient traffic flow (Mikulski 2010: 45). But driverless cars are no instant panacea for sound infrastructure design; existing road bottlenecks can create traffic congestion, even for driverless cars (American Highway Users Alliance 2015). Further, Fulton (from the University of California, Davis, Institute of Transportation Studies, cited in Muoio 2017) has drawn attention to the need for a system of road pricing even with driverless vehicles. He stated:

> [A]utonomous vehicles won't fix congestion woes unless a pricing system is put in place that discourages zero-occupancy vehicles ... We are especially concerned about zero-occupant vehicles that can happen with automated vehicles ... That scenario is especially plausible with private ownership of those vehicles and no limits to what we can do with them ... For example, many companies are interested in programming autonomous cars to run errands or pick up packages, but these efforts could increase traffic by multiplying the number of zero-occupant cars, or 'zombie cars' ... I think it's going to take some kind of pricing system that discourages zero-occupant vehicles and also makes penalties for single-occupancy vehicles.

Without a system of road pricing, it will also be difficult to incentivise a reduction of single-occupant vehicles on our roads. But this is predicated on people's willingness to share vehicles with others. Otherwise, the trend of single-occupant vehicles during peak traffic periods will not end with driverless vehicles. For example, Amman, the capital of Jordan (in the Middle East), has a two-tier taxi service. The more expensive service is a traditional book, hail and ride service, whereas the less expensive 'service'[2] taxis run on set routes with set stops, accepting passengers until the car is full. The resulting behaviours mean that rich people take traditional taxis and poor people take service taxis. Rather than efficiency, complex (or even superficial) ideas about class, taste, dignity and economic capacity can determine users' transport behaviours (see Veblen 1994). Studies of

---

2   In the French pronunciation of the word.

public transport have made similar conclusions: people are happy for governments to fund or subsidise public transport for others, but will continue to drive private vehicles for their own transport requirements (ARRB 2016; Carey 2016; Carrel et al. 2013).[3] And these trends are not necessarily consistent over time: a person living in high-density housing in Surry Hills in Sydney in the 1920s and catching the tram to work is a far cry, for example, from a person living in high-density housing in Surry Hills today and commuting on light rail. Where we live and how we travel have as much to do with trends, tastes and societal preferences as they do with efficiency and economy.

Increasing medium- to high-density inner-city housing means transport infrastructure such as bus and light rail services becomes less expensive for individuals as demand increases, and the shorter distances mean that transport infrastructure investment is more efficient, in that its supply, in a smaller geographical area, meets a concentrated demand. The preference for investment in light rail in Canberra, the Gold Cost, Sydney and Adelaide, for example, is based on the premise of higher-density housing located closer to where people work. While not necessarily requiring less investment in terms of infrastructure spending, transport infrastructure that serves a densely populated, discrete area enables greater potential return on investment due to high demand. For example, while a high-speed rail system between Melbourne and Sydney might enable people to live further from the central business districts, and the speed of the service ensures a shorter time for commuting, the return on investment depends on the number of people accessing the service from more distant places. Compare this with a light rail service in an area of high-density housing: the investment in light rail is less, but the demand for the service is considerably higher given the number of potential users of the service. For a high-speed rail service, which necessarily requires greater investment outlay, the consumer price for the service is considerably higher to achieve a commensurate rate of return on that investment. Given the potentially lower demand from a lower number of users in lower-density areas, there is a trade-off for the commuter in terms of the cost of using a high-speed rail service versus the cost of using a private car, but this may be offset by lower property prices. In terms of systemic efficiency, if light rail were to reduce the number of cars on inner-city roads then, paradoxically, there is an incentive for the use of private cars by those living outside the area serviced by light rail. So the *modal mix* becomes important in transport

---

3   For attitudes towards public transport in popular culture, see Jaffe (2015); The Onion (2000).

management, along with pricing and value capture or, alternatively, instances of policy tinkering in one area may create unforeseen behavioural problems in another.

The obvious trade-off with inner-city transport infrastructure is that property prices will increase in areas serviced by light rail, while properties further away from the CBD will remain less expensive. This means that, in the absence of alternative modes, less-wealthy people will continue to live further out and continue to rely on private vehicles, while wealthier people will enjoy the benefits of concentrated transport infrastructure, typically provided through public funding. This raises an issue of social equity, in that governments cross-subsidise the wealthy by providing transport infrastructure that does not service those who cannot afford to live in high-density, inner-city areas. Further, the road network that sustains those living in lower-density, outer-city areas is less efficient if it continues to be provided as a public good and will have little impact on transport behaviours unless alternative modes of transport are made available.

The hypothetical scenarios outlined above lead policymakers to consider two necessary interventions to capture these relevant externalities. First, some form of 'value capture' from improved land values is necessary to ensure that wealthier, inner-city property owners do not receive a free-rider benefit from increased property values brought about by public investment in transport infrastructure. Second, a form of discretionary road pricing is necessary to ensure that those who use the roads pay for that use. In the present system, behaviours become established in the absence of the true cost of externalities. A wealthy person can live in the inner city and take advantage of public transport, thereby reducing the individual's transport costs, whereas a less wealthy person would be better off living further from their place of employment and using their private car to commute. Such problems of equity make it difficult to balance social policy with economic policy outcomes. For Infrastructure Australia (2013: 17):

> The best approach to urban transport funding may be to source all funds directly from users or beneficiaries. The aim would be to encourage optimal travel behaviour and moderate demand, as well as provide finance for services and infrastructure. In an ideal world revenues would be higher than financial costs in order to account for externalities ... However, such an approach has not been adopted. Also, it may prove infeasible; for example in some circumstances it may be more efficient to collect taxes than user charges.

In the absence of appropriate pricing systems to 1) capture increased property values and 2) provide price signals for demand for transport infrastructure, there is little rational basis for investing in transport infrastructure other than for election purposes.

The path to road reform: A predilection for reporting, not acting

Three major inquiries relating to market reform, revenue reform and productivity have reported to the federal government: the Hilmer competition law review in 1993, the Henry review of tax in 2010 and the Harper review of productivity in 2014. In each case, the slow pace of reform, the lack of sustainability of the present funding arrangements and the inefficiency of the road transport sector (respectively) were noted. Further, many public submissions to the inquiries pointed to the road transport sector as an area of concern. The Hilmer review on competition law (Hilmer et al. 1993: 14) noted the progress on reforms such as those for rail and heavy vehicles while acknowledging that 'the community generally [was] impatient for much more rapid progress by governments in reforming our infrastructure and regulatory systems'. Road construction was not yet subject to consistent competitive tendering and Commonwealth–state cooperation on road transport was 'likely to be successful, though the pace of such cooperative effort [was] at times of concern' (Hilmer 1993: 209–10, 298). Further, Hilmer et al. (1993: 201) found 'a vast amount of regulation … [was] perceived to be restricting competition without adequate justification'. By the time of the Hilmer review, major market reforms were well under way in telecommunications (Dobes 1991), water (Tisdell et al. 2002: iii) and energy (AEMC 2017),[4] but, by comparison, the rate of reform of the road transport sector has been glacial.[5]

---

4   Energy sector reform began in 1991 and, in 1995, the Council of Australian Governments (COAG) endorsed the recommendations of the Hilmer review.

5   The Federal Interstate Registration Scheme (FIRS) for heavy vehicles (weighing more than 4.5 tonnes) began with the *Interstate Road Transport Act 1985*, and came into effect in 1987 as an alternative to state-based registration (DIRD 2017a). The purpose of the Productivity Commission's (2016) report was 'to assist COAG to implement efficient pricing of road and rail freight infrastructure' (see Chapter 9, this volume). But the harmonisation of national heavy vehicle laws was not consolidated until 2013, when the Heavy Vehicle National Law (HVNL) came into effect. Further, user charges for heavy vehicles based on actual use are still a few years away, with light vehicle user charges expected to take some 15 years (Fletcher, cited in Chang 2016).

The Henry review (Henry et al. 2010) found:

> Current road tax arrangements will not meet Australia's future transport challenges. (p. 53)

> ... Transport-specific taxes should only be imposed where they improve the way that people, businesses and governments make decisions. In general, this means that transport taxes should be designed to correct market failures in the transport sector. (p. 375)

> ... The existing structure of fuel tax, annual registration and other road-related taxes is designed primarily to raise revenue. These taxes more than cover the direct costs of providing road infrastructure, but are not capable of providing specific prices that vary according to location or time of use. (p. 376)

> ... Governments should analyse the potential network-wide benefits and costs of introducing variable congestion pricing on existing tolled roads (or lanes), and consider extending existing technology across heavily congested parts of the road network. Beyond that, new technologies may further enable wider application of road pricing if proven cost-effective. In general, congestion charges should apply to all registered vehicles using congested roads. (p. 377)

In 2014, the Harper review (Harper et al. 2015: 1) found that road reform was 'one of the top five issues most often raised in submissions', and it:

> recommend[ed] reforming road transport by introducing cost-reflective road pricing in a revenue-neutral way and linked to road construction, maintenance and safety so that road investment decisions are more responsive to the needs and preferences of road users. (p. 8)

Further:

> [I]n roads there has been little progress introducing pricing that reflects the actual cost of use on the network, such as time and location charging. Investment in those sectors is either funded directly from budgets or by users across the network rather than from users according to the costs they impose on the network. Roads in particular have also been subject to investment bottlenecks. (p. 194)

> ... [T]here has been little progress in attempting to introduce cost-reflective pricing in roads and linking revenue to road provision. As a consequence, there is criticism that new roads are being built in the wrong places for the wrong reasons, while too little attention is paid to getting more efficient use of existing road infrastructure. (p. 195)

Clearly, road pricing and provision are complex, but the reform process has been inordinately slow.

An interesting feature of the road transport sector in Australia is the immensely detailed and documented research and reporting that have occurred over the decades. Yet the Harper review (Harper et al. 2015: 38) found that 'roads are the least reformed of all infrastructure sectors, with institutional arrangements around funding and provision remaining much the same as they were 20 years ago'.

Given the extent of reporting on road reform over the years, from a policy perspective, it is surprising that progress has been so slow. For commuters in the major metropolitan centres, the daily realities of Australia's road networks should be enough to persuade any rational voter to call for change. But generational habits have a peculiar way of being hard to give up, as the Bureau of Transport Economics (BTE 1977: 147–8) discovered when considering road user charging (then referred to as 'cost recovery') some 40 years ago:

> The BTE's view is that private motor vehicle operation is essentially outside the framework of this study. This statement is not made merely to sidestep a difficult issue, but has sound philosophical grounds. In every other mode of transport, the major services are offered to the public through marketing agencies of various sorts (airlines, railways and so on). Whether such agencies operate at a profit or not is irrelevant in this sense. The fact is that such agencies form an identifiable interface between a complex background organisational structure and an individual user. The same applies for commercial road freight transport, where an end user of a transport service pays one fee to one organisation, and need not be aware of the complete organisational structure which leads to the setting of that fee. However, this system breaks down when private (i.e. not hire and reward) motor transport is considered. The private motor vehicle operator is, in many senses, on his own. In essence, he is a user of the road system, rather than a transport service.

The absence of point-of-sale pressure on road users' transport behaviours reinforces the status quo. This means reform is not a simple process, and yet another report will not make the transition any easier. But there has been some positive policy action that may see the long-overdue reforms placed firmly on the policy agenda.

Conclusion: A time for action

On 24 November 2016, Paul Fletcher, the Minister for Urban Infrastructure and Cities (2016a, 2016c; see also Chang 2016), announced that the Turnbull Government had committed to implementing five key initiatives of Infrastructure Australia's (2016) 15-year infrastructure plan. Further reform of heavy vehicle charges will be the priority, while the costs and benefits of a road user charging system for light vehicles will be investigated. The media release gave an indicative timeline of 10 to 15 years. This follows the minister's earlier call for submissions to a discussion paper on the wider use of value capture to fund infrastructure (Fletcher 2016b). Further, the minister echoed Infrastructure Australia's (2016: 87) words and agreed that public knowledge of the existing road funding regime is limited, with most citizens adverse to any form of charges, regarding them as a 'new tax'. Road reform will no doubt 'require the removal of familiar taxes and charges such as excise on fuel and registration fees' (Infrastructure Australia 2016: 87). At least a lack of research reports should not prove a stumbling block.

Public perception is the key issue affecting the ability of governments to be decisive in reforming this important productivity and revenue issue for Australia. Road pricing offers a 'doable' policy response to a major source of frustration for millions of Australians who experience traffic congestion every working day. The research has been done, the reports have been written, we have the technology and a consensus has formed among the key industry players. This is important: already the Australian Automobile Association is calling for changes to fuel receipts to show consumers how much tax they are paying at the pump (Coorey 2016). Yet the biggest challenge will be getting the states and territories on board. The states may baulk at yet another Commonwealth revenue grab after the experience of John Howard's legacy GST arrangements, or a 'GST birthday cake' may stall the process, and a lot will be riding on Minister Fletcher's recently announced 'eminent person' to champion the reform transition. Either way, finally, it appears that road reform is firmly on the political agenda.

References

American Highway Users Alliance. (2015). *Unclogging America's Arteries 2015: Prescriptions for Healthier Highways*. Washington, DC: American Highway Users Alliance. Available from: www.highways.org/wp-content/uploads/2015/11/unclogging-study2015-hi-res.pdf (accessed 2 August 2017).

Anthony, S. (2016). Super funds must boldly go where few investors will: 'greenfield' public infrastructure. *The Canberra Times*, 5 December. Available from: www.canberratimes.com.au/national/public-service/super-funds-must-boldly-go-where-few-investors-will-greenfield-public-infrastructure-20161129-gt01c7.html (accessed 1 August 2017).

Australian Bureau of Statistics (ABS). (2017a). *Australian National Accounts: National Income, Expenditure and Product, March 2017*. Cat. no. 5206.0. Canberra: ABS. Available from: www.abs.gov.au/ausstats/abs@.nsf/mf/5206.0 (accessed 1 August 2017).

Australian Bureau of Statistics (ABS). (2017b). *Engineering Construction Activity, Australia, March 2017*. Cat. no. 8762.0. Canberra: ABS. Available from: www.abs.gov.au/ausstats/abs@.nsf/mf/8762.0 (accessed 1 August 2017).

Australian Energy Market Commission (AEMC). (2017). *History of Energy Market Reform*. Sydney: AEMC. Available from: www.aemc.gov.au/about-us/history (accessed 3 August 2017).

Australian Road Research Board (ARRB). (2016). *Omnibus Survey Results: Congestion*. Research Report, 14 April. Melbourne: ARRB. Available from: cdn2.hubspot.net/hubfs/3003125/Major_Functions/PDF/ARRB%20Research%20report%20on%20congestion%20-%2014%20April%202016.pdf?t=1501211172699 (accessed 2 August 2017).

Bureau of Infrastructure, Transport and Regional Economics (BITRE). (2014). *Infrastructure, Transport and Productivity*. Information Sheet 55. Canberra: Commonwealth of Australia.

Bureau of Infrastructure, Transport and Regional Economics (BITRE). (2015a). *State of Australian Cities 2014–2015*. Canberra: Commonwealth of Australia. Available from: infrastructure.gov.au/infrastructure/pab/soac/files/2015_SoAC_full_report.pdf

Bureau of Infrastructure, Transport and Regional Economics (BITRE). (2015b). *Traffic and Congestion Cost Trends for Australian Capital Cities*. Information Sheet 74. Canberra: Commonwealth of Australia.

Bureau of Infrastructure, Transport and Regional Economics (BITRE). (2016). *Yearbook 2016: Australian Infrastructure Statistics*. Statistical Report. Canberra: Commonwealth of Australia.

Bureau of Transport Economics (BTE). (1977). *Cost Recovery in Australian Transport 1974–75*. Canberra: Australian Government Publishing Service. Available from: bitre.gov.au/publications/1977/files/report_033.pdf (accessed 15 January 2017).

Carey, A. (2016). Australian commuters would rather sit in traffic than on a train, survey finds. *The Age* [Melbourne], 13 April. Available from: www.theage.com.au/victoria/australian-commuters-would-rather-sit-in-traffic-than-on-a-train-survey-finds-20160413-go5lqw (accessed 2 August 2017).

Carrel, A., Halvorsen, A. and Walker, J. (2013). Passengers' perception of and behavioral adaptation to unreliability in public transportation. *Transportation Research Record: Journal of the Transportation Research Board* 2351: 153–62. doi.org/10.3141/2351-17

Chang, C. (2016). Turnbull Government considers new user pays system for cars. *News.com.au*, 23 November. Available from: www.news.com.au/finance/economy/australian-economy/turnbull-government-considers-new-user-pays-system-for-cars/news-story/0bab973c586f9a730e8695491138408f (accessed 3 August 2017).

Clark, R. G. (1988). Australian federal government road funding 1972–1986. *Australian Geographical Studies* 26(2): 279–94. doi.org/10.1111/j.1467-8470.1988.tb00579.x

Coorey, P. (2016). Transition to road user charge inevitable. *Australian Financial Review*, 24 November. Available from: www.afr.com/news/transition-to-road-user-charge-inevitable-20161123-gsw8i0 (accessed 4 August 2017).

Department of Infrastructure and Regional Development (DIRD). (2014). *Trends: Infrastructure and Transport to 2030*. Canberra: Commonwealth of Australia.

Department of Infrastructure and Regional Development (DIRD). (2016). *Trends: Infrastructure and Transport to 2040*. Canberra: Commonwealth of Australia.

Department of Infrastructure and Regional Development (DIRD). (2017a). *Federal Interstate Registration Scheme*. Canberra: Commonwealth of Australia. Available from: infrastructure.gov.au/roads/firs/index.aspx (accessed 20 July 2018).

Department of Infrastructure and Regional Development (DIRD). (2017b). *Roads to Recovery Program*. Canberra: Commonwealth of Australia. Available from: investment.infrastructure.gov.au/funding/r2r/ (accessed 3 August 2017).

Department of the Prime Minister and Cabinet. (1990). Transcript of joint news conference with the Hon. Bob Brown, Minister for Land Transport, Sheraton Hotel, Brisbane, 27 February 1990. Transcript ID 7931. Available from: pmtranscripts.pmc.gov.au/release/transcript-7931 (accessed 3 August 2017).

Desloires, V. (2016). Global infrastructure set for rerating as private equity dives in. *Sydney Morning Herald*, 26 October. Available from: www.smh.com.au/business/markets/global-infrastructure-set-for-rerating-as-private-equity-dives-in-20161025-gs9w7v.html (accessed 1 August 2017).

Dobes, L. (1991). The telecommunications reform process in Australia. *Telecommunications Journal of Australia* 41(1): 3–7.

Fitchett, T. K. (1976). *The Vanished Fleet: Australian Coastal Passenger Ships 1910–1960*. Adelaide: Rigby.

Fletcher, P. (2016a). Speech to the Sydney Institute, 16 August. Available from: minister.infrastructure.gov.au/pf/speeches/2016/pfs007_2016.aspx (accessed 15 January 2017).

Fletcher, P. (2016b). Government seeks public and industry input on value capture. Media release, 16 November. Available from: minister.infrastructure.gov.au/pf/releases/2016/November/pf078_2016.aspx (accessed 4 August 2017).

Fletcher, P. (2016c). Infrastructure Australia 15 year plan to guide key infrastructure policy directions for Turnbull Government. Media release, 24 November. Accessed 4 August 2017: paulfletcher.com.au/media-centre/media-releases/item/1842-infrastructure-australia-15-year-plan-to-guide-key-infrastructure-policy-directions-for-turnbull-government.html (site discontinued).

Goodwin, P. (2013). Peak travel, peak car and the future of mobility: Evidence, unresolved issues, policy implications and a research agenda, in *Long-Run Trends in Car Use*. Paris: OECD Publishing. doi.org/10.1787/9789282105931-en

Hancock, W. K. (1930). *Australia*. London: E. Benn.

Harper, I., Anderson, P., McCluskey, S. and O'Bryan, M. (2015). *Competition Policy Review: Final Report March 2015*. Canberra: Commonwealth of Australia. Available from: competitionpolicyreview.gov.au/files/2015/03/Competition-policy-review-report_online.pdf (accessed 12 August 2017).

Head, B., Wanna, J. and Warburton, J. (1990). *Implications of 'Fiscal Centralisation' for Public Sector Management in Australia.* Research Paper No. 11, February. Centre for Australian Public Sector Management. Brisbane: Griffith University.

Henry, K., Harmer, J., Piggott, J., Ridout, H. and Smith, G. (2010). *Australia's Future Tax System: Report to the Treasurer, Detailed Analysis Volume 2.* Canberra: Commonwealth of Australia.

Hilmer, F. G., Rayner, M. R. and Taperell, G. Q. (1993). *National Competition Policy: Report by the Independent Committee of Inquiry.* Canberra: Commonwealth of Australia. Available from: ncp.ncc.gov.au/docs/ National%20Competition%20Policy%20Review%20report,%20The%20 Hilmer%20Report,%20August%201993.pdf

Holderhead, S. (2017). Anger as SA 'dudded' in budget. *The Advertiser* [Adelaide], 10 May. Available from: www.adelaidenow.com.au/news/south-australia/ federal-government-shortchanged-sa-300-million-in-infrastructure-spending/ news-story/5119968fd765c773af3d38469184108d (accessed 3 August 2017).

Infrastructure Australia. (2013). *Urban Transport Strategy, December 2013.* Sydney: Infrastructure Australia.

Infrastructure Australia. (2015). *Australian Infrastructure Audit.* Sydney: Infrastructure Australia. Available from: infrastructureaustralia.gov.au/policy-publications/publications/Australian-Infrastructure-Audit.aspx

Infrastructure Australia. (2016). *Australian Infrastructure Plan: Priorities and Reforms for Our Nation's Future.* Sydney: Infrastructure Australia. Available from: infrastructureaustralia.gov.au/policy-publications/publications/Australian -Infrastructure-Plan.aspx

Infrastructure Finance Working Group (IFWG). (2012). *Infrastructure Financing and Funding Reform: Report Prepared by the Infrastructure Finance Working Group, April 2012.* Sydney: Infrastructure Australia. Available from: infrastructureaustralia.gov.au/policy-publications/publications/Infrastructure-Finance-Reform-Issues-Paper-Report-prepared-by-the-Infrastructure-FWG-2012.aspx (accessed 2 August 2017).

Jaffe, E. (2015). Buses are for other people. *The Atlantic*, January–February. Available from: www.theatlantic.com/magazine/archive/2015/01/buses-are-for-other-people/383513/ (accessed 2 August 2017).

Juturna Consulting. (2012). *Economic Reform of Australia's Road Sector: Precedents, Principles, Case Studies and Structures.* Juturna Consulting for Infrastructure Australia, February. Available from: infrastructureaustralia.gov.au/policy-publications/publications/files/Competition_Reform_of_the_Road_Sector.pdf (accessed 1 August 2017).

Laird, P. (2014). Australia's transport is falling behind on energy efficiency. *The Conversation*, 27 August. Available from: theconversation.com/australias-transport-is-falling-behind-on-energy-efficiency-29881 (accessed 1 August 2017).

Le Corbusier, C.-E. (1987 [1929]). *The City of Tomorrow and its Planning.* New York: Dover.

Mikulski, J. (ed.). (2010). *Transport Systems Telematics: 10th Conference, TST 2010, Katowice—Ustron, Poland, October 20–23, 2010. Selected papers.* Berlin: Springer. doi.org/10.1007/978-3-642-16472-9

Muoio, D. (2017). Why self-driving cars could be terrible for traffic. *Business Insider*, 5 June. Available from: www.businessinsider.com.au/self-driving-cars-traffic-congestion-2017-6 (accessed 2 August 2017).

Newman, P. (2015). Don't panic! Traffic congestion is not coming for our cities. *The Conversation*, 27 July. Available from: theconversation.com/dont-panic-traffic-congestion-is-not-coming-for-our-cities-45154 (accessed 3 January 2017).

Newman, P. and Kenworthy, J. (2011). 'Peak car use': Understanding the demise of automobile dependence. *World Transport Policy & Practice* 17(2): 31–42.

Organisation for Economic Co-operation and Development (OECD). (2010). *Economic Survey of Australia 2010.* Paris: OECD.

Organisation for Economic Co-operation and Development (OECD). (2012). *Economic Survey of Australia 2012.* Paris: OECD.

Organisation for Economic Co-operation and Development (OECD). (2014). *Economic Survey of Australia 2014.* Paris: OECD.

Organisation for Economic Co-operation and Development (OECD). (2017). *Economic Survey of Australia 2017.* Paris: OECD.

Organisation for Economic Co-operation and Development (OECD) and International Transport Forum (ITF). (2013). *Long-run trends in car use.* Round Tables, No. 152. Paris: OECD Publishing/ITF.

O'Rourke, J. (2015). Toll war revs up: Sydney drivers face congestion tax or road user-pay system. *Sunday Telegraph*, 12 July. Available from: www. dailytelegraph.com.au/news/nsw/toll-war-revs-up-sydney-drivers-face-congestion-tax-or-road-user-pay-system/story-fni0cx12-1227438090226 (accessed 12 July 2015).

Pigou, A.C. (1920). *The Economics of Welfare*. London: Macmillan.

Productivity Commission. (2016). *Road and Rail Freight Infrastructure Pricing*. Report No. 41. Canberra: Productivity Commission.

Saleh, L. (2015). Editorial: Nothing tolls for me. *Sunday Telegraph*, 12 July.

Standing Committee on Infrastructure, Transport, Regional Development and Local Government and King, C. (2008). *Rebuilding Australia's Coastal Shipping Industry: Inquiry into Coastal Shipping Policy and Regulation*. Canberra: Parliament of Australia. Accessed 28 April 2017: www.aph.gov. au/House/committee/itrdlg/coastalshipping/report.htm (site discontinued).

Sturgess, G. (1996). Virtual government: What will remain inside the public sector? *Australian Journal of Public Administration* 55(3): 59–73. doi.org/ 10.1111/j.1467-8500.1996.tb01223.x

The Age. (1954). States' answer to Privy Council ruling: Rail commissioners to hold conference. *The Age* [Melbourne], 29 November, p. 3.

The Onion. (2000). Report: 98 percent of US commuters favor public transportation for others. *The Onion*, 29 November. Available from: www. theonion.com/article/report-98-percent-of-us-commuters-favor-public-tra-1434 (accessed 2 August 2017).

Tisdell, J. G., Ward, J., Grudzinski, T. and Cooperative Research Centre for Catchment Hydrology. (2002). *The Development of Water Reform in Australia*. Melbourne: CRC for Catchment Hydrology.

Veblen, T. (1994 [1899]). *Theory of the Leisure Class*. Mineola, NY: Dover.

Vickrey, W. (1948). Some objections to marginal-cost pricing. *Journal of Political Economy* 56(3): 218–38.

Vickrey, W. (1963). Pricing in Urban and Suburban Transport. *American Economic Review* 53(2): 452–65.

Webb. R. (2004). *Commonwealth Road Funding since 1990*. Research Paper No. 7 2003–04. Canberra: Parliamentary Library. Available from: www. aph.gov.au/About_Parliament/Parliamentary_Departments/Parliamentary_ Library/pubs/rp/rp0304/04rp07

Section 2: Long-term planning

3

Reforming transport planning in Australia

Marion Terrill

This chapter considers ways to reframe transport planning in Australia by reorienting debate away from the traditional investment-only focus on big projects to considering transport as an organic enabling system interconnected with many spheres of policy. To date, most transport planners have been preoccupied with planning how people should move about as if they are in control of the system. Planners have devised various ways to move people and freight around more efficiently, including approaches such as 'park and ride', carpooling, avoiding peak hour, utilising freeways, avoiding 'rat-running' and requirements for delivery trucks to deliver at night. All of these approaches have one thing in common: they are attempts to work out what people should be doing and planning how they should move about.

Planning a complex social system is difficult, but it does not stop people from trying to do it. We see this in a lot of different fields. I will address transport planning shortly, but first let me discuss how any complex social system works and how it organises itself. There is a fierce debate going on at present about science and maths training. We have people such as Australia's Chief Scientist saying we need to lift enrolments for core science disciplines at post-secondary levels. We have the Business Council of Australia saying we need to devise a 10-year plan to get more students into tertiary science and technology courses. Their voices are not alone, but we could ask another set of questions: why are so many people choosing courses other than science and technology; why are they making the 'wrong choices'; and, who is managing the education system?

The reality is that no one is managing it. People are making their own decisions. The system is organising itself. People are deciding whether to study science and maths, or fashion, or fine art, or law, or nothing at all, on the basis of their own preferences, what they think they will do at the end of it and what they have to pay directly and indirectly. If we do not have enough science and technology graduates, those who do these disciplines will command a higher wage, we will import graduates from countries such as Ireland or China, or people in related fields will upskill. Meanwhile, those people who have studied fashion and fine art are presumably doing a thing they value more, even if getting a job at the end of it is harder. Therefore, our ability to really manage these systems and to get people to do what we want is pretty limited. So, what I want to do in terms of framing is to say that when society tries to solve these complex social problems, the best thing to do most of the time is to try to create the right incentives, then it is not necessary to plan the precise details, as people will figure out what to do and how to adapt to situations.

The concept of the self-organising system is incredibly relevant to transport planning. It is very clear that we need ports and roads and trains, and that government has an important role in ensuring we have the means to move around and that freight can get to and from airports, warehouses and depots. But how do we decide how many we need and where to put these things? This chapter is about how we approach this question. I will discuss the four major levers that are available to government in its transport planning role: investment, pricing, regulation and network management.

As with government, I will start with the investment function. So much of the public debate about transport planning begins and ends with investment. We have recently witnessed former treasurer Joe Hockey invoking the spirit of Joh Bjelke-Petersen as he welcomed the appearance of 165 cranes over the Sydney CBD and even two springing up in Hobart. Meanwhile, in the lead-up to the Canning by-election in Western Australia in 2015, federal opposition spokesman on transport and infrastructure, Anthony Albanese, talked about the government's neglect of infrastructure and how dire that neglect is for increased congestion.

In an environment of population growth, it is clear there will need to be growth in infrastructure investment, even if the exact nature of what is needed is a lot less clear. So the aspect of investment I will discuss here—which is one that seldom receives much airtime—is the issue of timing. I will start by mentioning a really important marker in the business environment today: the cheapness of money. Yields on 10-year government bonds hit an all-time low in February 2015, of 2.28 per cent. In other words, it has never been cheaper for government to borrow money—not just in Australia, but also around the world. Andy Haldane (2015) from the Bank of England has found that short-term interest rates are at their lowest point since Babylonian times. Money is cheap. If ever there was a time to borrow for transport infrastructure, now is that time.

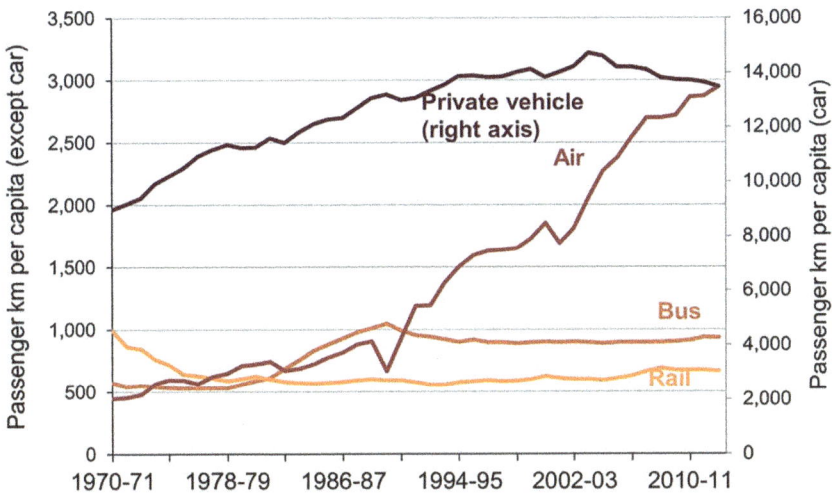

Figure 3.1 Domestic passenger travel per capita
Sources: BITRE (2015: Table T3.1, p. 61); ABS (2014a).

On the other hand, demand for transport infrastructure is changing. Figure 3.1 indicates passenger demand for different types of transport on the basis of per capita distance travelled. It is immediately apparent that the distances people are travelling have flattened, and are beginning to decline slightly after years of growth—most evident in private vehicle travel. Use of other transport modes has increased, but overall domestic distance travelled per capita is 1 per cent lower than it was 10 years ago. The volume of domestic freight per capita has increased reasonably steadily over the past 20 years. It did flatten a bit at the time of the Global Financial Crisis (GFC). And there has been quite an increase in the past decade, but it has come mainly from rail, and that has been mainly bulk rail in Western Australia—in other words, iron ore. Moving to an aggregate level, and taking account of population growth running about 1.4 per cent at last count (ABS 2016c), passenger car travel is now levelling off, air travel is still booming and bus and rail are growing more slowly. The volume of domestic freight has continued to increase in aggregate.

This suggests that population growth alone is not a reliable indicator of investment need, given the changing nature of travel demand across the modes.

Another consideration, as indicated in Figure 3.2, is the level of existing investment. This shows that while government spending has recently slowed, it remains well above the level of 2004, when current rapid growth began. The figure indicates that the value of engineering construction work completed and the value of transport infrastructure building over the past decade have in fact been the highest since the Australian Bureau of Statistics (ABS) began collecting this information. They peaked in 2012, but declined over the next two years. There is some GFC stimulus spending included in the figure; nevertheless, the level of investment over the past 10 years has been considerable.

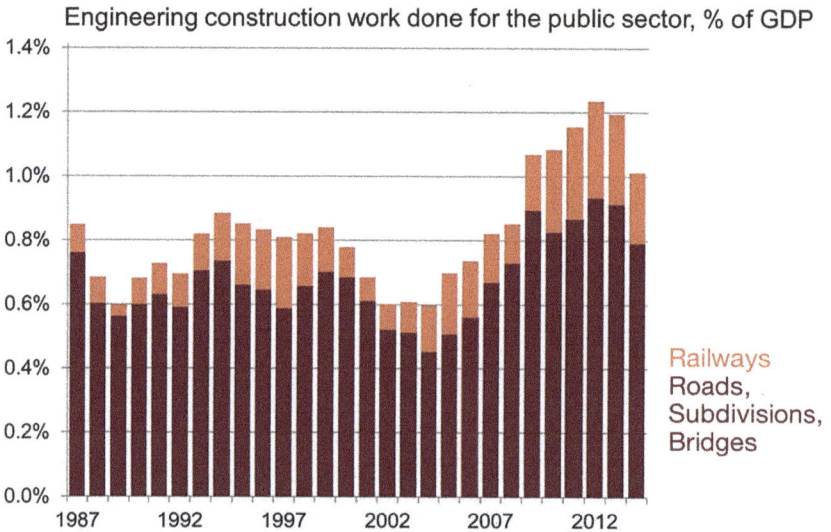

Figure 3.2 Government spending on transport infrastructure
Sources: ABS (2016a; 2016b: Table 11).

Why does it matter today that governments have spent so much in the past decade? It matters because of the debt that is now sitting on state and territory balance sheets for that spending. Over the seven years to 2013–14, interest and depreciation costs as a percentage of state revenue increased from about 6 per cent to 9 per cent, and are estimated to remain close to 9 per cent over the forward estimates period, as Figure 3.3 indicates. Interest expenses have increased more quickly than depreciation. The increase is equivalent to states spending about 0.5 percentage point of gross domestic product (GDP) more to cover the infrastructure spending of previous years, and this is despite extremely low interest rates.

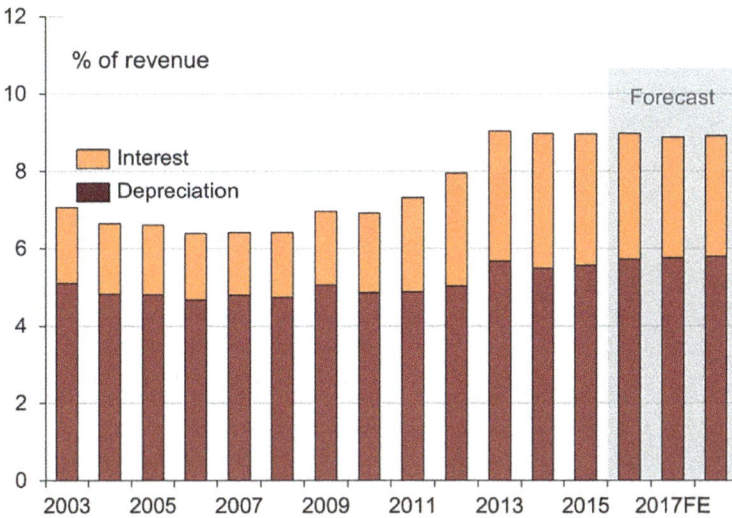

Figure 3.3 State and territory depreciation and interest costs
Source: ABS (2014b), cited in Grattan (2014).

So what should Australian governments do about their transport investment? The states are taking a range of very different positions. The Victorian Treasurer, Tim Pallas, made headlines by contemplating debt financing public infrastructure (Davey 2015), and largely on the basis that Victoria's 10-year borrowing rate is 2.65 per cent—close to the cheapest it has ever been. The Queensland Government has indicated that it may be prepared to borrow money to fund needed public transport infrastructure if the Commonwealth does not help (APP 2015), and that is essentially because Queensland is not participating in asset recycling. On the other hand, the NSW Government has brought forward $600 million of infrastructure spending, because it is benefiting from a stamp duty windfall from the Sydney housing boom as well as $20 billion from electricity privatisation (Gerathy 2015). Western Australia is pushing back its investment program, with its iron ore royalties dropping precipitously (Government of Western Australia 2015: 5).

In summary, my reading of the situation is that governments have built a great deal of infrastructure over the past 10 years, and that has corresponded with the mining boom. However, state governments have essentially competed for construction resources in that time. Now that private investment is falling, the public sector has already committed to substantial transport infrastructure construction and is not especially well placed to take advantage of this buyer's market; therefore, this does not seem to have been the wisest way to run infrastructure policy. On the other hand, one might say, 'What is done is done, and what should we do now?' It is very clear that we should still be open to funding transport infrastructure if there is a good cost–benefit ratio; admittedly, this is a big 'if'.

Turning to the second lever—pricing—the biggest issue is road pricing, and it is hard to spend much time in transport circles without coming up against this issue. Expert opinion from the Henry review and the Productivity Commission to the Harper review has all lamented the inefficient way we fund and manage our roads. Road pricing is essentially about explicitly charging for the costs that one vehicle's road usage imposes on others. Typically, this focuses on one of two things: the cost of maintenance due to wear and tear (and this relates largely to heavy vehicle usage) and the cost of congestion to regular users and potentially other externalities. This concerns all vehicles in particular places and at particular times.

The congestion argument may be summarised as follows: when people suffer in bumper-to-bumper traffic, they conclude that we need to build more highway lanes; but when governments reflexively add capacity to solve congestion, it helps, but only temporarily. Before long more traffic builds up, and once again we are trying to solve the same problem. A study in the United States found worsening congestion in 99 of 100 places studied since 1994, even though in 92 of those places there was an increase in the amount of roadway miles per capita. In fact, building more roads to try to move vehicles faster can make traffic worse. Focusing on the 'rush-hour peak' also ignores the much greater availability of the road system in 'off-peak' periods, when far greater numbers of trips could be taking place. The potential value of moving some trips off peak is high. Nevertheless, such road-building strategies can also occur at the same time as a relative underfunding of public transport, which ironically leads people to rely more on private cars because of poor performance or services in public transport networks.

An interesting case involving the introduction of road user charging has occurred over the past decade in Stockholm, Sweden. One of the architects of Stockholm's congestion charging, Jonas Elliasson, sought explicitly to counter the fear that ministers feel about congestion charging by careful consideration of the rollout of the scheme. There were four major findings from this Swedish experiment.

First, a very modest initial charge in a trial period can make a big difference to acceptance. In Stockholm, the charge of €1 to €2 for people to travel to Stockholm's CBD reduced traffic in a heavily congested area by 20 per cent, with people's response immediate and rather pronounced. Second, the experiment found that the relationship between traffic flow and congestion is not linear; a reduction of 20 per cent in vehicle numbers would reduce congestion by far more than 20 per cent. Third, surveys found that people in Stockholm were fiercely against the pricing program at first, with reports of up to 70 per cent opposition. However, by the time the trial was conducted, this had reversed—to 70 per cent in favour of the pricing program. What this means in terms of transport planning is that 70 per cent of people in Stockholm wanted to pay for something that had previously been 'free'. Fourth, experts found that road users adapted their attitudes and behaviour so thoroughly they could not even remember what they used to believe; they thought they had supported congestion charging all along!

My reflection on this experiment is that we should not assume that congestion pricing is impossible. The experience overseas suggests that governments in Australia are far too timid. Given that the pay-off from congestion pricing has the potential to be very high, we could achieve much more functionality in transport usage with much less political pain than the political class fears. I suggest the most useful message is that we should get on with convincing them of the benefits of congestion charging.

The third lever is regulation. Transport regulation generally has the objective of enabling the best use of scarce resources in moving people and things around, and, in more commercial settings, this typically means at the lowest cost. But regulation does not always lead to cost containment. I will cite two examples of 'skewed' regulation that focus partly on the objectives of transport accessibility, but also bring in other political objectives that may ultimately determine the regulatory settings: ports and ride-sharing.

Ports play an important, if not particularly obvious, role, with the cost of port services an important component of the cost of goods and services, which ultimately falls on either consumers or exporters. There are several ways that regulations affecting ports could be improved.

First, when ports are put up for sale or long-term lease, state governments should avoid the temptation to inflate the sale price without retaining control of ongoing user charges. In Melbourne recently, the Australian Competition and Consumer Commission (ACCC) made a forceful submission to the Victorian Legislative Council on legislation before the Victorian Parliament to lease the Port of Melbourne on a 50- to 70-year lease (ACCC 2015). As the ACCC emphasised, governments have a strong incentive to structure their privatisation process to maximise the sale price, but this price—if it is high—will flow through to port users into the future. In fact, the ACCC went so far as to say that the government's privatisation policy could be considered to effectively impose a tax on future generations of Australians. The government has proposed a 50- to 70-year lease with price controls for the first 15 years, but, after that, the process remains unclear.

Second, governments should minimise the fees charged to ports and port operators. Between 2012 and 2016, there was a $75 million licence fee for the Port of Melbourne—which, in other words, is a tax on trade. Fees and charges like this are simply passed on. The chief executive officer (CEO) of freight logistics company Asciano, John Mullen, has said: 'If a port owner has to put up prices to try and get a return, ultimately the consumer, or manufacturers, or exporters are paying that bill' (Roberts 2014). Similarly, the Port of Melbourne recently imposed a rent review on one of its stevedores, DP World, asking for a staggering 767 per cent increase in the rent it pays, leading to a bitter dispute (Financial

Review 2015). The firm currently pays $16 to $18 per square metre. Following the dispute, the firm will now be paying $20 per square metre, rather than the proposed $120.

A third improvement that could be made to the regulations affecting ports is shipping regulation. The Commonwealth could overturn the current rules that make it perfectly legal for groupings of two or more shipping lines to band together and charge what is known as pan-Australian freight rates. Under such arrangements, shipping companies charge the same rate at each port of call, meaning there is no incentive for the more expensive ports to bring their costs down, and there is no advantage to running a lean operation. Effectively, this means the leaner ports are subsidising the less efficient ports. These types of changes would lower the input costs of businesses that want to export and the costs of goods that go to Australian households and businesses. Therefore, there are potential benefits to be gained in regulating ports.

My second example is ride-sharing through companies such as Uber— currently very topical. During 2015, taxi and hire car operators were planning rolling 24-hour strikes and rallies across the major cities in Australia. Most of the debate about Uber and ride-sharing more generally focuses on taxi regulation. The Victorian taxi industry has experienced more reforms than elsewhere. Taxi regulations cover four key areas: safety, availability, customer service and price. While it is likely that all states over time will narrow the gap between ride-sharing and taxis, it is not clear how long this will take. Nevertheless, the biggest barrier is likely to be the value of perpetual licences, which governments have issued over the years and which are essentially a right to operate a taxi. In Melbourne, taxi licences have traded at about $290,000, and in Sydney, $390,000 (Taxi Services Commission 2017; RMS 2017).

Figure 3.4 indicates that passengers are already voting with their feet. I have taken data from the United States, where ride-sharing is a little more established than it is here, and what you can see is the first panel shows the steady drop in the number of taxi trips taken in San Francisco, with the introduction of transport network company regulation making little or no difference to the trend. Similarly, in Australia, despite the uncertain legal status of Uber, in its first six months of operation, 11 per cent of Sydney residents used the service. It has only become more popular since then; the price is competitive and many people believe it offers better customer service.

Taxi revenue and licence values fall sharply once ride-sourcing takes off

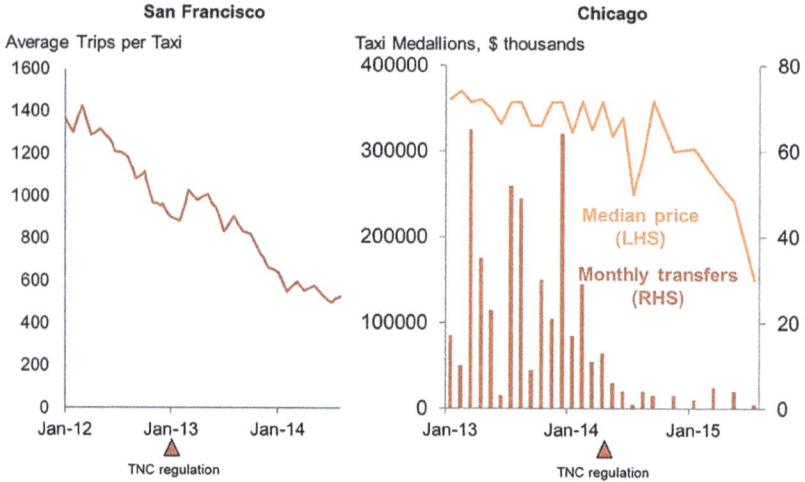

San Francisco

Chicago

Average Trips per Taxi

Taxi Medallions, $ thousands

Median price (LHS)

Monthly transfers (RHS)

TNC regulation

TNC regulation

Figure 3.4 Impact of ride-sharing on taxi revenue and licence values
Note: TNC = transportation network companies.
Sources: Chicago Data Portal (2018); DataSF (2018).

The right-hand panel in Figure 3.4 shows what happened in Chicago to the price of 'taxi medallions', which are similar to Australia's perpetual licences. It is likely a similar drop could be experienced in Australia. The Independent Pricing and Regulatory Tribunal (IPART) in New South Wales (NSW) has estimated that 15–20 per cent of the price of a taxi fare is being transferred to the licence owner as economic rent. While taxi regulation is really important to Uber, it is not the only kind of regulation that matters. There are two other important elements: tax and employment law. On tax, Uber is taking the Australian Taxation Office (ATO) to court over whether even occasional ride-share drivers should register for the goods and services tax (GST), with Uber arguing its drivers are members of the sharing economy and should be treated the same as Airbnb hosts, who do not have to register for GST until their turnover reaches $75,000 a year. On the other hand, the ATO is saying, 'You are providing taxi services, so you have to pay it from the first dollar, as taxis do.'

On employment law there has been recent publicity in the United States concerning a San Francisco judge who ruled that Uber drivers in California were employees, which opens the door to benefits such as overtime pay and reimbursement for expenses. Here in Australia, this issue is not entirely clear. It is arguable that Uber drivers are more like contractors in the sense that they choose how much work, if any, they do, and they do not wear a uniform or have a livery. Further, the GST decision indicates that they are regarded more like contractors. Uber does set rates of pay and drivers can drive for Uber only if they are authorised to use its app. This is still very much a 'grey' area.

What does all this mean for transportation regulation? Getting more trips from the existing cars on the road does improve capital productivity. Enabling people to work—including having people who would have worked just a little or just a little more than they do at present—is employment boosting. This is good for the individual, they are good for the economy and there is no compelling reason not to establish the minimum sufficient regulation to give ride-sharing the scope to operate legally. The only sticking point is the political problem of the declining value of perpetual taxi licences, and this really depends on how courageous governments are prepared to be.

The fourth and final lever available to government is network management. This is a low-glamour, but high-return, lever. Figure 3.5, compiled by Infrastructure Australia, reports an enduring finding. A similar finding came out of the Eddington Transport Study in the United Kingdom. It is that small and medium-sized projects tend to have higher benefit–cost ratios than many of the mega projects that are so appealing to so many governments.

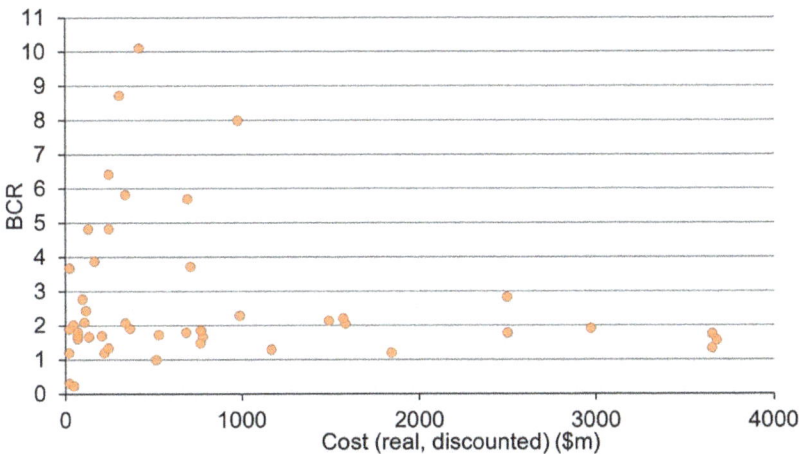

Figure 3.5 Economic returns of smaller schemes compared with larger schemes (projects submitted to Infrastructure Australia)

Note: BCR = benefit–cost ratio.

Source: Infrastructure Australia (2013).

An example of this is Melbourne's rail network. This network is not particularly small, but close to $1 billion has been spent on maintenance and renewal over the past four years—after what has been described as decades of neglect. There are a few issues here. One is the outdated signalling, which is a big source of delays in the system. Some signals are 100 years old, with a design life of much less than this. They are prone to failure, they are expensive to maintain and there are few people left who know how to maintain them.

Similarly, the network includes some very complex rail junctions. What this means is that a failure or delay on one part of the track cascades through the network. As the different lines converge on to the city loop, throughput is limited by the capacity of the loop, and where lines converge the speed is limited to 25–40 kilometres an hour. This is an important facet in the relatively poor performance of the Melbourne network during peak periods.

A third problem is a lack of adequate electrical power, particularly in the inner city. All trains bought this century have had to be detuned to perform to the same specifications as the older and slower trains, which require less voltage. The newest trains perform very badly under this low voltage. These impediments are not small things, but they are also not mega projects, and so are not so appealing to politicians in terms of the publicity opportunity. But they are not about building new things so much as about getting more from existing assets. This is also a prominent focus in NSW, where the state is spending $1 billion on upgrades to the existing road network, including works to relieve congestion at pinch points across the capital, Sydney, to extend clearways, make improvements to real-time traffic management and so forth.

In a similar vein is the issue of maintenance across the entire transport network. It is difficult to make general comments about the overall state of maintenance of Australia's transport network, but Figures 3.6 and 3.7 are indicative.

Australia's investment in transport infrastructure is high…
% of GDP

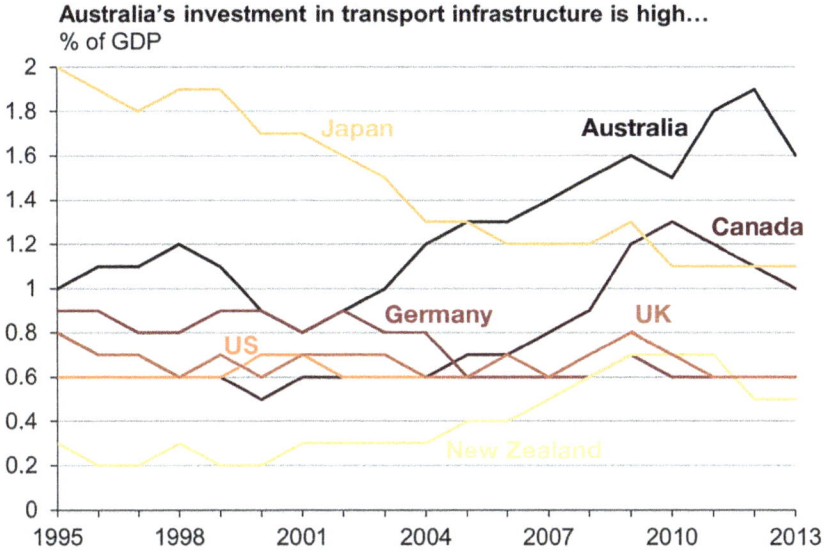

Figure 3.6 International comparison of Australia's investment
in transport infrastructure

Source: OECD (2016).

… unlike our spending on maintenance
% of GDP

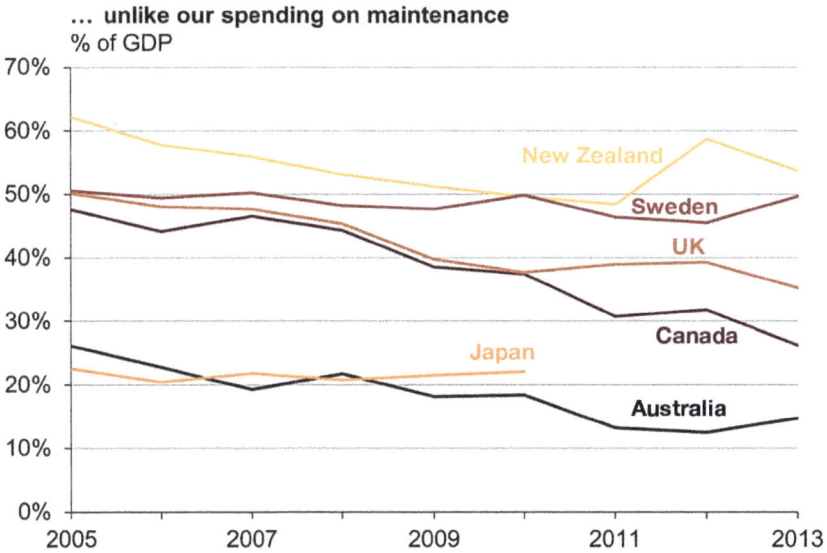

Figure 3.7 International comparison of Australia's maintenance
expenditure on transport infrastructure

Source: OECD (2016).

Figure 3.6 shows that, from 2004, (new) Australian investment in transport infrastructure increased dramatically, and it remained at very high levels compared with other Organisation for Economic Co-operation and Development (OECD) countries. On the other hand, Figure 3.7 shows our maintenance spending on transport infrastructure seems to be at the bottom of the pack of OECD countries. Without being a comprehensive study, this suggests our maintenance spending—or maintenance activity—may not be keeping up with our new building; and perhaps we are more keen to build new infrastructure than to look after what we already have. Essentially, the points to be made about network management are that we should 'sweat' the assets, we should be open to small and medium investments as well as big ones and we should set the maintenance budget with some reference to the value of the underlying assets.

Conclusion

Our thinking about transport planning is best when we set the broad structure of the system, but avoid trying to determine the detail of how we want businesses and individuals to respond. In this chapter, I have argued that in relation to transport planning the challenge is to push back from an investment-only focus and a desire to build big, heroic projects. Transport, after all, is an enabling service; it is not something we generally value in its own right. We value it as it enables us to do other things that we care about. This means it does not really have its own agenda, but is part of many other agendas.

We should remember that we have at our disposal not just the investment lever, but also three other important levers, which should be fully exploited in creating the transport system: pricing, regulation and network management. In the meantime, the message for policymakers is to stop counting cranes on the skyline.

References

AAP. (2015). Labor will break debt promise: Qld oppn. *News.com.au*, 12 June. Available from: www.news.com.au/national/breaking-news/borrowing-would-break-promise-qld-oppn/news-story/0501932a17791fc9c950c24512 339ad1 (accessed 20 July 2018).

Australian Bureau of Statistics (ABS). (2014a). *Australian Historical Population Statistics*. Canberra: ABS. Available from: www.abs.gov.au/ausstats/abs@.nsf/mf/3105.0.65.001 (accessed 20 July 2018).

Australian Bureau of Statistics (ABS). (2014b). *Government and Finance Statistics, Australia, 2012–13*. Cat. no. 5512.0. Canberra: ABS. Available from: www.abs.gov.au/Ausstats/abs@.nsf/0/51DE444E27EF9358CA257E4300 117E05?OpenDocument (accessed 20 July 2018).

Australian Bureau of Statistics (ABS). (2016a). *Australian National Accounts: National Income, Expenditure and Product, December*. Cat. no. 5206.0. Canberra: ABS. Available from: www.abs.gov.au/ausstats/abs@.nsf/mf/5206.0 (accessed 4 April 2017).

Australian Bureau of Statistics (ABS). (2016b). *Engineering Construction Activity, Australia, Dec 2015*. Cat. no. 8762.0. Canberra: ABS. Available from: www.abs.gov.au/Ausstats/abs@.nsf/0/B464AA38E5436D56CA257FE 000173850?OpenDocument (accessed 20 July 2018).

Australian Bureau of Statistics (ABS). (2016c). *Regional Population Growth, Australia, 2014–15*. Cat. no. 3218.0. Canberra: ABS. Available from: www.abs. gov.au/ausstats/abs@.nsf/Previousproducts/3218.0Main%20Features402014-15?opendocument&tabname=Summary&prodno=3218.0&issue=2014-15&num=&view= (accessed 20 July 2018).

Australian Competition and Consumer Commission (ACCC). 2015. *ACCC submission to the inquiry into the proposed lease of the Port of Melbourne*. 10 September. Available from: www.accc.gov.au/system/files/ACCC%20 submission%20to%20the%20inquiry%20into%20the%20proposed%20 lease%20of%20the%20Port%20of%20Melbourne_0.pdf (accessed 20 July 2018).

Bureau of Infrastructure, Transport and Regional Economics (BITRE). (2015). *Yearbook 2015: Australian Infrastructure Statistics*. Canberra: BITRE. Available from: bitre.gov.au/publications/2015/files/BITRE_yearbook_2015 _full_report.pdf (accessed 4 April 2017).

Chicago Data Portal. (2018). Public passenger vehicle licenses. *Chicago Data Portal*. Chicago: City of Chicago.

DataSF. (2018). Website. Available from: datasf.org/opendata/ (accessed 20 July 2018).

Davey, M. (2015). Victoria's economy 'strong enough to handle debt to fund infrastructure'. *The Guardian*, 27 August. Available from: www.theguardian. com/australia-news/2015/aug/27/victorias-economy-strong-enough-to-handle-debt-to-fund-infrastructure

Financial Review. (2015). DP World wins rent battle with Port of Melbourne. *Financial Review*, 3 August. Available from: www.afr.com/business/transport/ dp-world-wins-rent-battle-with-port-of-melbourne-20150803-giqddz (accessed 20 July 2018).

Gerathy, S. (2015). NSW budget 2015: Six things we already know. *ABC News*, 22 June. Available from: www.abc.net.au/news/2015-06-22/nsw-budget-2015-six-things-we-already-know/6562326 (accessed 20 July 2018).

Government of Western Australia. (2015). *2015–16 Budget: Economic and fiscal outlook*. Budget Paper No. 3, May. Available from: www. parliament.wa.gov.au/publications/tabledpapers.nsf/displaypaper/3912914 acf7f3f5176e784f348257e45002d38a5/$file/2914.pdf (accessed 20 July 2018).

Grattan Institute. (2014). *Budget Pressures on Australian Governments*. Melbourne: Grattan Institute.

Haldane, A. (2015). Speech to the Open University, 30 June. Available from: www.bankofengland.co.uk/-/media/boe/files/speech/2015/stuck.pdf?la= en&hash=3247D34307D99E8E4E11E5B890837AD6C6CAEFFB (accessed 20 July 2018).

Infrastructure Australia. (2013). *Infrastructure Australia's submission to the Productivity Commission Inquiry into Public Infrastructure — Submission.* December. Available from: infrastructureaustralia.gov.au/policy-publications/ publications/IAs-submission-to-the-Productivity-Commission-Inquiry-into-Public-Infrastructure-Submission.aspx (accessed 20 July 2018).

Organisation for Economic Co-operation and Development (OECD). (2016). *Transport: Infrastructure Investment*. Paris: OECD. Available from: data.oecd. org/transport/infrastructure-investment.htm (accessed 4 April 2017).

Roads & Maritime Services (RMS). (2017). *Sydney Metropolitan Transport District taxi licence transfers: January 2008 – October 2017*. NSW Government. Available from: www.rms.nsw.gov.au/about/corporate-publications/statistics/ public-passenger-vehicles/licence-transfers/sydney.html (accessed 20 July 2018).

Roberts, G. (2014). Port privatisations hurt economy: Asciano. *Sydney Morning Herald*, 7 May.

Taxi Services Commission. (2017). *Metropolitan taxi-cab licence transfer prices: 1 September 2015 – 31 January 2017*. Victoria State Government. Available from: taxi.vic.gov.au/__data/assets/pdf_file/0003/18192/Licence-Transfer-Values.pdf (accessed 20 July 2018).

4

How to deliver better infrastructure planning

Philip Davies

Soon after the delivery of the speech on which this chapter is based, Infrastructure Australia (2016) released its 15-year Australian Infrastructure Plan.

The plan was developed following consultation on the Australian Infrastructure Audit and recommended fundamental changes to the way Australia plans, funds, delivers and uses its infrastructure.

It had 78 recommendations for reform and was structured around four main themes:

- productive cities, productive regions
- efficient infrastructure markets
- sustainable and equitable infrastructure
- better decisions, better delivery.

Alongside the plan, Infrastructure Australia released a new Infrastructure Priority List, which identified 93 projects and initiatives around the country. The list provides rigorous, independent advice to governments and the public on the infrastructure investments Australia needs.

Infrastructure Australia will update the plan at least every five years and the priority list regularly throughout each year.

For more information and to download the plan and the priority list, go to www.infrastructureaustralia.gov.au.

The public discussion on infrastructure is often constrained by focusing on specific projects, rather than long-term policy and strategy, and there are certainly some challenging opportunities in front of us—not least those identified in Infrastructure Australia's recent audits. We see growing population levels, and the recent audit suggests we could face an annual cost of traffic congestion of $53 billion by 2031. We also have governments grappling with budget constraints and long-term environmental concerns. On the other hand, we are seeing continued economic growth and an increase in demand for infrastructure services—and most of these are good signs. These are signs of the success of the nation; however, unless we engage with some of these challenges now, we are going to wake up in the future and realise our quality of life is not what it used to be.

Auditing existing practices and demand projections

This chapter focuses on the importance of long-term integrated planning, particularly the integration of transport and land use planning. As a starting point, I will take the opportunity to set the scene somewhat in terms of what my organisation, Infrastructure Australia, does and what our role is in providing leadership. Infrastructure Australia's role includes being an advisor to governments, as well as to investors and owners of infrastructure, through the whole life cycle of their assets, but particularly around policy and planning. In mid-2014, with bipartisan support, the *Infrastructure Australia Act* was amended, setting up Infrastructure Australia as an independent statutory body with a mandate to prioritise and progress nationally significant infrastructure. The Act also established a 12-person board and the right to appoint a CEO. I was appointed in 2015, and we were already in the throes of some fairly significant activity relating to planning, including the release of the Northern Australia Audit and the Australian Infrastructure Audit, both released in May 2015. Both documents highlighted the need for action and provided an evidence base from which to build our future plans.

The Australian Infrastructure Audit in particular took a long-term view, out to 2031. It considered some of the key drivers of demand and identified some of the challenges we will face if we do not act (it is very much about if we do not act); this evidence base is what we have now drawn on, working closely with states and territories, to start to identify some of the solutions we think will address the challenges. These issues were brought together in the 15-year Australian Infrastructure Plan, which was released in 2016.

One of the key findings of the Australian Infrastructure Audit was that, after 2031, we are likely to face an increase in population of 40 per cent—to about 30.5 million people, as indicated by Figure 4.1. At present, our population—to put it into context—is the fastest-growing among the members of the Organisation for Economic Co-operation and Development (OECD). Most of that population growth is forecast to be in our four largest capital cities: Sydney, Melbourne, Brisbane and Perth. Figure 4.2 indicates the projected growth of these four cities. There are two questions we have to ask ourselves. First, what does the increase in population in our cities mean for how these cities will operate and function? This is an important question because the major cities are projected to grow, by 2061, to a size comparable with London, New York and Paris today. This means we need to think differently about how our major cities operate. Second, what are the outcomes we want, and are there opportunities to grow some of the smaller capital cities in a different way so we can spread the load and make better use of the infrastructure we already have in those cities?

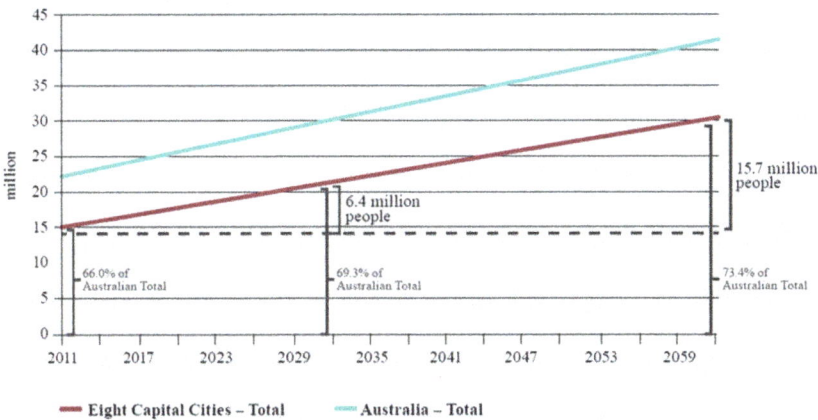

Figure 4.1 Australia's projected population growth to 2061

Source: Infrastructure Australia analysis of data from ABS (2013a; 2013b: Series B).

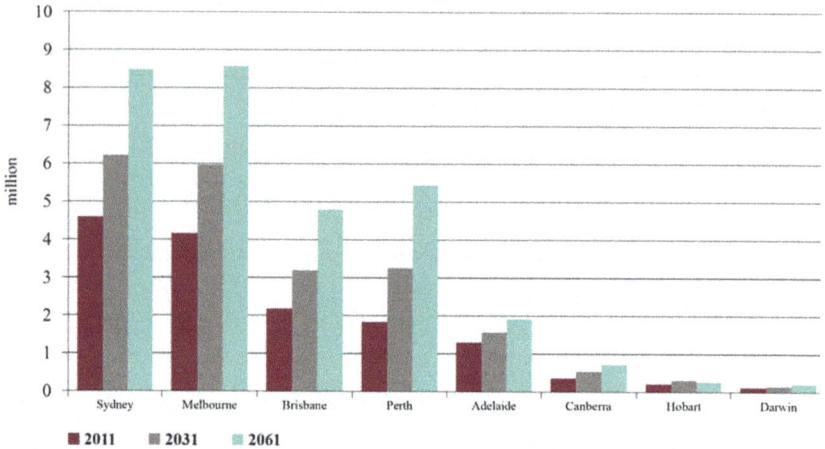

Figure 4.2 Projected population growth in Australian capital cities to 2061

Source: Infrastructure Australia analysis of data from ABS (2013a; 2013b: Series B).

Reiterating the need for long-term planning

It is crucial we embrace this opportunity to shape and plan not only our cities, but also our future infrastructure needs. This is not an easy role. It is fair to say we have moved away from long-term planning in recent years and have become very focused on the short term—largely on major projects. We need to get back to basics with regard to strategic planning, at the regional, city and national levels. More so than in the past we are seeing a great deal of change, such as demographic change, with an ageing population, shifts in the patterns of demand and much disruption, which is spoken about a lot—but not all of this disruption is bad. Most of us appreciate that this disruption presents a great opportunity, particularly to connect with the community and take them on a journey. We are seeing global economic shifts and changes in the way we go about doing our work. Unfortunately, despite the importance of these challenges, long-term planning is missing somewhat, and our project pipelines are relatively short. Addressing these issues is the call to arms we have picked up, along with our colleagues, around the country in developing this 15-year plan.

We have identified a number of key trends. One is that, in Australia, we have moved away from planning and feasibility studies. These were a big feature in the past, but are not so much a feature today. We have also moved, on occasion, to committing funding to problems before they are turned into solutions and fully developed as projects. We have also not had enough focus on getting the most out of the infrastructure we already have—something touched on in the previous chapter. One of the things Infrastructure Australia is focused on, therefore, is the better use of what we already have, before we rush off to plan a new project. Yet, as a result of this lack of a pipeline, we in Australia are not consulting enough with the community. Often our conversations come very late in the piece and do not bring the community on the journey. Currently we are undertaking a small number of post-completion reviews, which often highlight that our previous infrastructural projects appear to be examples of lost opportunities. Ex-post reviews give us the insight into the outcomes that were delivered, so we can learn from our good work as well as our bad work and feed that back into the next project.

Some of the benefits of long-term planning tend to run counter to the abovementioned points, and a return to long-term planning will help address many of the major issues we face. We must recognise that projects generally cannot be delivered overnight; they take years of planning before we can give them a green light and have them ready to proceed. A return to long-term planning at the state and federal levels means we will have an observable long-term pipeline of up-and-coming projects. To date, the general absence of that pipeline of projects has meant the supply chain has also suffered, so it is not just about the people involved in delivering these projects within government; it is also about the downstream supply chain. Without a long-term pipeline, suppliers are not able to plan their resources and their capability, and employers are not sure whether they should recruit, retain or train staff, especially in some specialised areas. Subsequently, Australian taxpayers pay the cost for that.

Improving our planning capabilities

There are a number of key areas for improvement in planning. First, there is real need for higher-quality data to underpin our decision-making, and this is certainly something we found while conducting the Australian Infrastructure Audit. Access to data is still a challenge. Second, there is much discussion about integrated land use and transport planning— or integrated land use and infrastructure planning—yet it does not happen. In particular, we have moved away from protecting transport corridors.

Third, there is a growing need for greater transparency and rigour in our project selection processes. Fourth, as mentioned above, there is a need for ongoing ex-post reviews, as these provide learning opportunities.

In terms of data, we have certainly seen a lack of quality across most sectors. We found in the audit that it was particularly challenging to collect data on the operations and maintenance of assets, the performance and delivery of infrastructure, the services and service levels the infrastructure is delivering and the cost of maintenance. As Marion Terrill argues in Chapter 3 (see Figures 3.2 and 3.6), we are investing a lot in infrastructure, but perhaps not paying enough attention to how much we need to be spending on maintenance and operations. This may sound somewhat pessimistic, but we are not alone in facing these challenges. The most recent period has been about supporting the mining boom, building up our infrastructure and getting the country going; and, in such circumstances, it is unnatural to focus on sweating assets and driving performance improvements. So, this is not a problem we have; it is more a matter of shifting our focus.

I previously worked in the United Kingdom, with responsibility for operating London's roads, and, despite the levels of congestion in London and the challenges there, we had exactly the same issues. The maintenance funding would often be spent on things other than maintenance. For instance, there were about 6,000 traffic signals in the city and, when I took over responsibility, no one had looked at timing the traffic signals for some 27 years. In effect, they were installed and subsequently forgotten about. London at the time was a city going through significant growth and experiencing significant congestion, with a good deal of pressure to address those issues. But it had not been done because it was not the focus of the times. I use this example as a kind of baseline to show that we know we are not alone in this; we just need to shift our focus.

Having said that, another area we could improve on is thinking about systems and networks. We need to gain a better understanding of how infrastructure actually works together (intermodally). When we are project focused, it is easy to avoid thinking about the bigger picture, how the solution fits into a network and how we can make the system work as a whole. When looking at pieces of a supply chain, it is important to consider the whole chain. With these challenges in mind, our 15-year plan has some suggestions about how we might address them.

In terms of the evidence base, we found some gaps in data availability, but what we did do well in the audit was some detailed modelling, particularly around some of the transport corridors in our capital cities. We looked at what that estimated $53 billion worth of congestion actually looked like in terms of transport corridors. That has certainly been very helpful in the planning process on which we have embarked with the state and territory governments—looking at what the solutions might be and then using those to inform the plan. And, in the interests of sharing access, we have made our assembled data available to all. There is now an awful lot of data on our website if anyone is interested in looking at it, and some regional development agencies have already been using it for their own planning purposes. Obviously, we need to build this evidence base over time, and that is something Infrastructure Australia has been talking with the Commonwealth Department of Infrastructure about.

Integrated transport and land use planning is an important function that can be improved. And it is not just about moving people; it is also about moving goods. Infrastructure Australia's audit predicted that we will see a doubling of land freight volume to 2031. Particularly around some of the larger capital cities, we are approaching circumstances similar to something I experienced in the late 1990s in Japan, where there was a 'game change' in terms of how goods were distributed around Tokyo. Although Tokyo is a much larger city than any of Australia's capital cities hopefully will ever be, there was a real shift in terms of how goods were distributed through the city, and that is the type of thinking we need to adopt here.

What we tend to find today is that the planning and provision of infrastructure and land use are still often undertaken in silos, with different government departments responsible for different aspects of the infrastructure network in terms of its planning and delivery, and, as a result, we do not necessarily get the outcomes we need or deserve—and that is one of the reasons we do not think at the systems level. Therefore, we are very focused on how we think about planning. On occasion, our cities are not planned in the best way, and in the context of the growth we are expecting, this is something to which we really need to pay attention.

As a first step in long-term planning, we are looking to work closely with state and territory governments, where we can play a role in challenging how we think about planning as we bring this 15-year plan together. Another thing we have done well in the past, but not so well recently, is to protect transport corridors—one of the benefits of which is that we can accommodate future projects at a reasonable cost. History demonstrates that corridor protection is an important element of long-term planning.

Between the 1950s and the 1980s, a number of state governments protected corridors that enabled major projects to be built, such as the West Link M7 in New South Wales, the East Link in Victoria and, in recent times, the Badgerys Creek Airport site in Sydney. Many of these sites were set aside some 10 to 20 years before the project commenced. So there is evidence that state governments have had some success in long-term planning, but corridor protection has often been overshadowed by a short-term focus in recent times.

Another area of discussion is the transparent project selection process; and, once having done a good job of the long-term planning, it is important to ensure we have a rigorous process for evaluating our projects and that our projects are adequately solving the problems we need to solve. Options to solve some of these problems need to be appropriately identified and scoped, and we do not need to attempt a new solution all the time; we also need to be thinking about how we can improve what we already have. For example, would new signalling on a rail system actually provide greater benefits than building a new rail line?

Infrastructure Australia's strategic advisory role

Infrastructure Australia is required to undertake an assessment of all projects of national significance over $100 million for which Commonwealth funding is sought. Despite what some people think, we do not develop our own business cases and we do not make decisions regarding the funding of projects. Our role is that of an advisor and an assessor of the solutions presented, and hopefully we have been involved in developing these solutions early in the piece, where we can provide useful input and advice. We do assess the cost–benefit of projects, we make those assessments public once they are completed and we have a rigorous methodology for conducting the assessment. We look at strategic fit—how that solution fits into the wider network—how it addresses the problems of national significance that have been identified, at the evidence that has been provided and at the economic viability. Importantly, the proposal must have a clear delivery plan and be deliverable and realistic.

In terms of oversight, the Department of Infrastructure plays an important role. Once Infrastructure Australia has completed its strategic planning role, the department will often oversee the project when it is to receive federal funding.

An area where we in Australia really could do better is in assessing the outcomes of projects. Once the planning and implementation of the project are complete, it is crucial that we measure the outcomes, understand whether we delivered the benefits in the business case and the broader outcomes of some of our investments, in terms of not only the project, but also its impact on the community and its fit into a system or a city or wherever it might be. These outcome assessments are necessarily long term in their approach. We might measure these things when we implement a project, we might need to measure them five years later, 10 years later or so on, and without that kind of evidence it is difficult to improve the way we do our planning; this is something on which we need to focus.

Having discussed many of the challenges and some of the improvements in planning we could make, what has Infrastructure Australia's role been in supporting some of these processes? We are keen to play our role—from both an advisory and a facilitation point of view—and we must get back to building and maintaining the evidence base, we must return to long-term integrated planning and we must start to secure corridors, not only *in* our cities, but also *between* them, and we must ensure there is a transparent, rigorous project selection process, and that we get back to doing ex-post reviews.

Infrastructure Australia is focusing on these matters, and we are committed to provide more commentary on the issues in the wake of our 15-year plan. The plan was structured around four themes:

• productive cities, productive regions
• efficient infrastructure markets
• sustainable and equitable infrastructure
• better decisions, better delivery.

This planning process was not conducted in isolation, as we worked closely with our colleagues in the infrastructure agencies, organisations, governments and industry bodies across the country—focusing particularly on the long-term agenda. During the consultation process in which we travelled around the country talking about the audit, we have consulted with more than 500 people, including representatives of private organisations and governments, to seek their input into shaping this future plan.

We also met separately with state and territory governments to work together to solve some of the challenges we identified in the earlier audit to feed information into the plan. We received more than 85 submissions to the plan that helped inform our decisions; we have begun updating our Infrastructure Priority List and we have refreshed the way we consider projects as part of that process.

Conclusion

The main driver on which we need to focus at present is the scale of projected population change, which is something we have not seen before, particularly in our four largest capital cities. If we get this right, however, we can protect and enhance the quality of life we all enjoy. Infrastructure Australia must play a key role in supporting our collective long-term planning into the future. The plan we released in 2016 represents a major step forward in taking a solid evidence base and developing solutions to protect Australia's infrastructural future.

References

Australian Bureau of Statistics (ABS). (2013a). *Australian Demographic Statistics: March Quarter 2013*. Cat. no. 3101.0. Canberra: ABS. Available from: www.abs.gov.au/AUSSTATS/abs@.nsf/Lookup/3101.0Main+Features1Mar%202013?OpenDocument

Australian Bureau of Statistics (ABS). (2013b). *Population Projections, Australia, 2012 (base) to 2101*. Cat. no. 3222.0. Canberra: ABS. Available from: www.abs.gov.au/AUSSTATS/abs@.nsf/DetailsPage/3222.02012%20(base)%20to%202101?OpenDocument

Infrastructure Australia. (2016). *Australian Infrastructure Plan: Priorities and Reforms for Our Nation's Future*. Sydney: Infrastructure Australia. Available from: infrastructureaustralia.gov.au/policy-publications/publications/Australian-Infrastructure-Plan.aspx

5

Singapore's land transport management plan[1]

Teik Soon Looi[2]

This chapter explores Singapore's system of land transport management, describing what we have done and why. As many international observers have noted, Singapore is often regarded as a global exemplar for its management of the city-state, but transport management involves very complex issues and we have had to 'shift the debate' in our own jurisdiction to achieve sustainable change.

I begin by asking how Singapore fares today. We have just celebrated 50 years of nation-building since independence. We are a compact city-state with one level of government, unlike Australia, which has a federal government and different states and territories. This makes things easier for us—decision-making is faster and centralised—but it also brings problems, which I will share. Our population is 5.5 million and still growing. Our land area is limited and housing already consumes 14 per cent and roads a further 12 per cent of the available land mass. We realised some time ago that we cannot go on building roads; this is a reality we had to face.

---

1   All data and figures used in this chapter come from the Land Transport Authority, Singapore.
2   The views expressed herein are the author's responsibility and may not reflect the views of the Land Transport Authority, Singapore.

Singapore has changed enormously over the past 50 years, from a city of congestion and overcrowded, unreliable buses in the 1960s and 1970s to an efficient, sustainable urban transport system today.

So how did we do it? First, we put public transport at the core. We also made a deliberate choice to make public transport affordable, comfortable and reliable; and we wanted public transport to be viable or financially sustainable for the long term.

The statistics on our high-density transport system tell us that 7.7 million trips are taken daily—comprising 1 million taxi trips, close to 3 million rail trips and close to 4 million bus trips every day. The rail-based rapid transit system remains the backbone of the transport system, supplemented by the bus system. Buses provide comprehensive coverage, with more than 350 routes and 4,552 buses in operation. We now have three bus service providers or operators, including two longstanding large operators, SMRT Buses and SBS Transit. In addition, we recently opened up the industry through a competitive tender process and the third provider, Tower Transit, started operation in early 2016. Bus fares and services are regulated as we transition to a bus service contracting model over the next two years.

Rail transport is the backbone of our system because it offers high-capacity rapid travel along the major corridors. Today we have two operators, SMRT Trains and SBS Transit. We retain two operators because we believe in competition and want to do benchmarking comparisons of performance. Our rail system is still expanding; we started with 67 lines, we now have 182 and we are going to double that to 300-plus. Again, fares and services are regulated, and we have a competitive tendering regime in place to allow operators to compete for operating licences for rail services.

Figures 5.1 and 5.2 indicate how we compare against other major cities in terms of usage and convenience of buses and rail, as well as our preference for public transport and low private car ownership (in terms of private cars per person and measured against gross domestic product (GDP)). These indicate that Singapore (circled in red) is unusual in many ways, especially compared with Sydney and Melbourne (shown circled by broken lines).

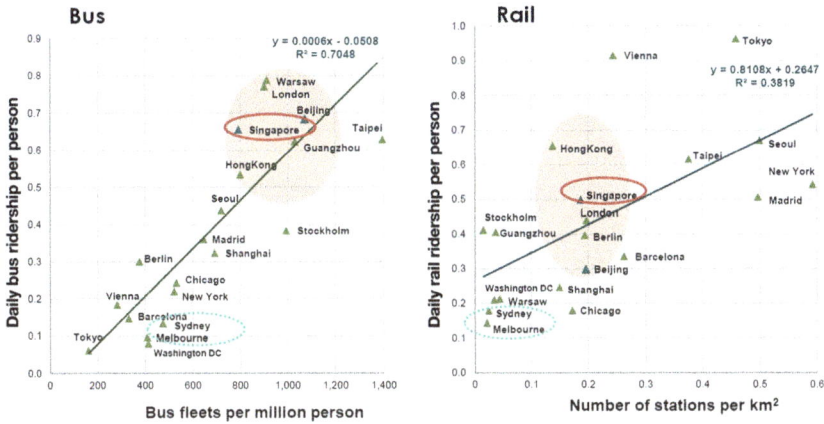

Figure 5.1 Public bus and rail usage

Source: Local Transport Authority, Singapore.

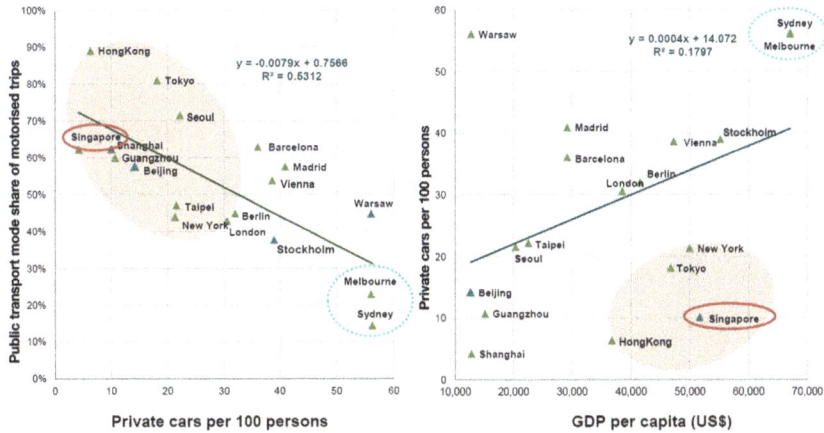

Figure 5.2 Mode sharing versus private vehicle use

Source: Local Transport Authority, Singapore.

Singapore's standing on these charts is a result not of chance, but of judicious planning and sound policy interventions. In Singapore, we control the growth of the number of vehicles and vehicle usage, and we have congestion pricing as a major component of traffic demand management. After Hong Kong, Tokyo and Seoul, Singapore is one of the heaviest users of public transport—and, again, Melbourne and Sydney are outliers.

But we still have challenges. Our population is projected to grow from 5.5 million to 6.9 million by 2030—a figure we use for infrastructure planning. In undertaking future planning, we have to know the size of the market for which we are going to cater, so this expected increase in population is one of our key challenges. As mentioned, our land area is limited, so there are many competing demands and many trade-offs are necessary. We often try to design multiple uses for strategically located land (surface use as well as aerial and underground uses), which requires us to debate with the city planning authorities on land use allocation when we are planning transport facilities. We have to design our system to be commuter-centric and not planner-centric; people have changing needs and preferences and they seek to be engaged in decision-making. This desire for greater engagement has been raised in commuter surveys quite frequently in recent years. Another challenge we face is the issue of whether to operate public transport enterprises on a for-profit basis or on a desired performance basis. We are quite market driven in the provision of public transport services and the operations are profitable. But we have been debating how we can better balance the issue of profitability vis-à-vis the kind of performance the community wants to see—a kind of social obligation that may be expected from these public transport service providers.

Planning for transport management

So how do we plan in practice? In transport planning, our strategy is to use integrated land use and transport planning based on a 'hub and spoke' concept. It is quite straightforward (Figure 5.3). We have dormitory towns and new (or Housing Development Board (HDB)) towns where people live, and we service these with local feeder buses, which link to transport hubs and on to longer journey corridors, including the commute into the central city. We bring people via the feeder 'spokes' to the hub, and then into the city. There are great efficiencies here. We also use buses on long-haul journeys in corridors that are not yet served by mass rapid transit (MRT) trains. The most important thing here is that the transfers are seamless, and we focus on taking care of the first and last mile of the transport journey to complete commuter convenience.

HDB Towns   **Transport Hub**   **City**

- **Feeder/MRT journeys**
- **Long-haul journeys in corridors not yet well served by MRT**
- **Serve local needs or short journeys**

Bus **MRT**

- **Make transfers seamless and take care of first-mile last-mile**

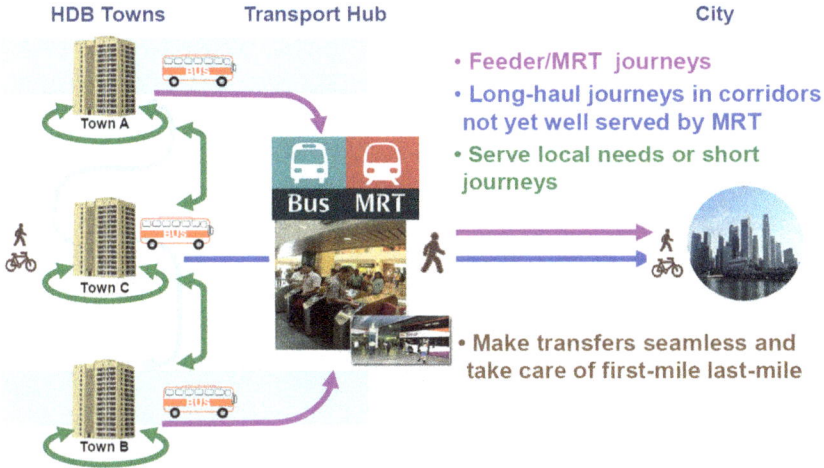

Figure 5.3 An integrated hub-and-spoke network
Source: Local Transport Authority, Singapore.

Our overall concept dates back to the 1970s; we refresh the plan every 10 years, with the latest plan now developed for 2030 and beyond. Much of the central planning is coordinated by five key government agencies. The Land Transport Authority (LTA) is in charge of all land transport matters, while the Urban Redevelopment Authority (URA) is the central city planner. The Housing Development Board plans housing estates or towns, the Jurong Town Corporation (JTC) develops industrial and business parks and the National Parks Board is in charge of making Singapore a city in a garden. With these key players in the government's service, it is easier to organise coordination. Not that we don't have problems; it is just that coordination becomes easier because these are the largest determiners of transport and land use planning parameters.

We believe a strategic long-term view is very important. Our planning horizon is 30 to 40 years, supplemented by mid-term master plans running out to 10 to 15 years. The near-term plans run for five to 10 years and are sometimes called planning feasibility studies. From these cascading plans, we in the LTA develop our rolling five-year road development program, the rail lines master plan and the bus network plan.

I have been asked many times: why does Singapore do such long-range planning? There are three main reasons. First, such planning makes economic sense as it helps us to maximise 'value capture' in the system. Because we plan ahead, we can promote high-density transit–oriented development, optimise our land take and enhance overall system viability. Second—and probably most importantly—we can shape the travel patterns of commuters in terms of meeting transport demand with supply, and we can provide more travel options and reduce car dependency through better transport interconnectivity. Third, we also get the chance to safeguard our plan for future transport corridors by making provisions such as setting aside land and connecting facilities.

Let me provide two examples, which those who have been to Singapore may have seen in operation. Sengkang Town transport hub is a high-quality integrated development. It has good connectivity and transport choices: Light Rail Transit (LRT), heavy rail or MRT, buses and taxi drop-offs for passengers. Another example is the giant interchange facility at Dhoby Ghaut—something like one might see in Hong Kong or Tokyo. With five underground levels, the station connects three rail lines (the north–south, north–east and circle lines). Costing some S$268 million (A$259 million) and opened in 2003, it was among the first integrated transport hubs. The LTA developed a substantial commercial property above the station, including an 18-storey office tower, to capitalise on the value capture.

In planning transport facilities, we can be very obsessive about minimising the land take. As a road planner, every time I proposed adding an extra lane, I would be asked: 'Why are you doing that? If you don't need that, don't do it! If you take one more lane, it's less space for others, the shop frontages may have to go, the green planting strips will go.' In the planning authority, we have a mechanism called the Master Planning Committee, which brings different agencies together to deliberate on land use allocations and to discuss options and trade-offs.

Land transport master plan

In the LTA, we have had three major planning rounds: 1995–96 saw our first white paper produced (the LTA was formed in 1995); in 2008, we revised the plan and called it the 'Land Transport Master Plan (LTMP) 2008'; and we issued a further LTMP in 2013. We are well into the 2013 LTMP and are talking about the next version, due in late 2018. The five-year plan keeps changing because circumstances change quickly and we have to anticipate and plan ahead, as transport facilities are lumpy projects that take time to be realised. Currently, we have a set of clear objectives aimed at enhancing the travel experience. These objectives are more connections, better service, liveable inclusive communities and a reduced reliance on private transport. These are then supported by specific and measurable targets to drive transport management: 75 per cent of journeys to be made on public transport; 85 per cent of journeys of less than 20 km to be completed in less than 60 minutes; and 80 per cent of households living within a 10-minute walk from a train station. These targets paint the picture, and we have to deliver them by 2030.

More connections

In terms of increasing connections, our rail network has expanded to more than 150 km, and we are building more rail lines very aggressively. The rail network is becoming denser in terms of the interconnectivity of rail corridors, the latest being the Downtown Line, which will be completed in stages, from the north-west to the city centre and extending further to the east.

We have not forgotten buses, however. During the 1980s, when we were opening many new rail lines, we questioned whether we should discard or curtail bus routes because of the efficiency of rapid rail transport. We used the term 'bus service rationalisation', and reduced bus routes to avoid duplicating the rail lines and used them as feeders to the train stations. We are now returning buses to some corridors because they offer more choice, and people still want them.

Greater interest has also emerged in 'active mobility'—more walking and more cycling, especially for the first and last mile of a journey. Singapore is a tropical city, so we are building a lot of covered walkways through the 'walk2ride' program. These ideas are gaining a lot of traction and public acceptance and we are looking at how best to engage people and promote such movement.

Better service

As we expand our rail facilities, we also need to consider renewing and enhancing the existing network. Presently, we are changing our signalling systems to add capacity in terms of allowing more train trips. But we cannot build train lines overnight to meet immediate demands. Train lines are lumpy infrastructure and take about six to 10 years to be realised. So, while waiting for new lines to be built, we have decided to ramp up our bus services. Through the Bus Service Enhancement Program (BSEP) launched in 2012, an additional 1,000 buses were added to do three things: improve connectivity in the interim, ease crowding and increase reliability. Besides adding more buses to increase capacity and create new services, we also introduced the Quality Incentive Framework, using market mechanisms to incentivise the operators to do better. This idea, taken from London, sees operators encouraged to overperform to gain additional payment for services, while, if they underperform, their service payment will be reduced.

While we have the BSEP in place, we need market signals to tell us whether the operators are efficient and whether we (and consumers) are paying the right price for the services. We are therefore moving to a bus service contracting model. We announced this decision in 2014; we introduced the first of two bus service contracting packages in 2015, which gave us some price information for the third package, awarded in 2016. Such information will enable us to negotiate with bus operators as we transition the remaining packages into the contracting model.

Another measure we have introduced is to shift behaviour in terms of managing peak demand. Peak-hour travel is always going to be a problem, but one way to deal with it is to incentivise commuters to travel outside peak hours—for example, by offering free travel before morning peak times. In economic terms, we are experimenting with the 'power of free' to change commuter behaviour. Currently, we offer free rides if commuters arrive in the city from selected stations. If commuters exit the stations before 7.45 am, they qualify for a free ride; they receive a discount on the normal fare if they are just outside that time (7.45–8 am). Leveraging on our ticketing system—which is a closed system using 'tap in/tap out' monitoring—we have implemented a scheme called the Travel Smart Reward, which allows commuters to earn points, much like a loyalty program. Off-peak travellers can play a game and win prizes, and this has proven to be a successful innovation.

Liveable and inclusive community

In terms of inclusivity, we have been making our trains and buses more accessible to the aged and people with disabilities. We recognise that Singapore has an ageing population who will need assistance with access. We also have to educate other transport users about the needs of our elderly or disabled communities—even with simple things such as pedestrian crossings that are designed to make drivers slow down and give way to those seeking to cross.

Reducing reliance on private transport

In relation to private transport, we have sought to change the narrative from 'I want a car' to 'why would I want a car?'. This is a real challenge, but it will eventually be achieved. Some years ago, when I visited Copenhagen, the 'cycling city', I asked locals, 'Would you ever consider owning a car?' The question had not even occurred to them. They said: 'Why would I want to own a car? Cycling is fine by me.' So, in Copenhagen—even with a lower population density than Singapore—locals do not seek to own cars and prefer bike riding. In contrast, Singapore, with its higher density, has developed public transport as our preferred strategy to reduce private car ownership and congestion.

We control vehicle ownership through the vehicle quota system, which has been in place since 1991. As can be seen from Figure 5.4, we have significantly cut the rate of growth in vehicle ownership through use of the quota system. If a person wishes to own a vehicle, they must place a bid in a public auction for a Certificate of Entitlement (CoE), and only if they are successful can a vehicle be bought. As the supply of CoE reduces in tandem with controls on the vehicle growth rate, the auction price increases. Today, Singaporeans have to pay about S$70,000 (A$67,600) just to secure a piece of paper entitling them to buy a car—an increase from S$10,000 (A$9,700) in the mid to late 2000s—while the quota of new CoEs has fallen from 2,500 per bidding exercise to just 500. The cost of a CoE is therefore two to three times the price of a medium-sized car.

To further constrain vehicle usage, we use Electronic Road Pricing (ERP), which began as a manual Area Licensing Scheme (ALS) in 1975, and has been in place since 1998, when the technology became available. Our system is a usage charging system based on a cordoned area and a point along a road. One of the benefits of going fully electronic was that it eliminated the need to staff the gantries to check on vehicles passing through. Our narrative with this policy is very clear: ERP is about congestion pricing; it is not about collecting tolls for road maintenance or repair.

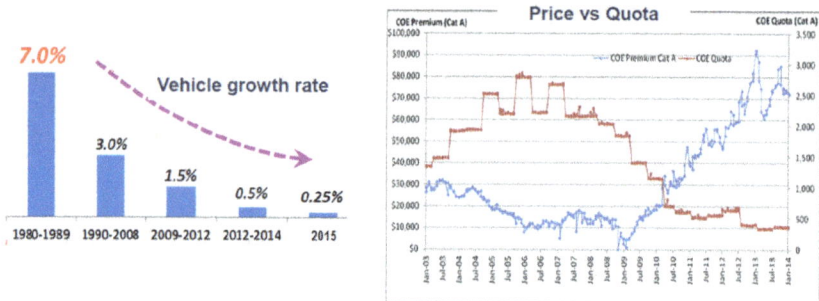

Figure 5.4 Ownership restraint: Vehicle quota system
Source: Local Transport Authority, Singapore.

Setting the appropriate ERP rate is very important. Our rates vary according to the time of day and location. Rates will increase or decrease depending on whether the speeds along the road are more or less than the defined speed ranges, as illustrated in Figure 5.5. We review the charges every three months. This is to ensure we are setting the right price signal. Motorists can read the amount to be charged every time they pass through the ERP gantries, with each deduction accompanied by a sound effect that reminds the driver they are paying for that trip.

- ERP rates reviewed every 3 months
- 85% of motorists assured of smooth travel within the optimal speed ranges

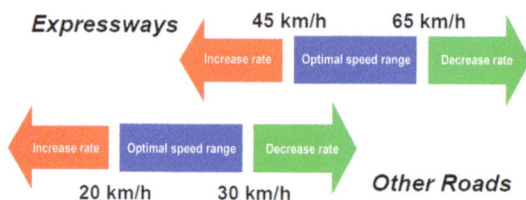

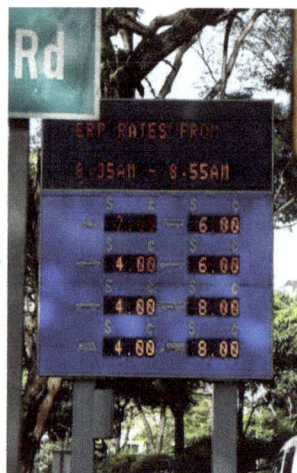

Figure 5.5 Spatial and temporal flexibility in Electronic Road Pricing
Source: Local Transport Authority, Singapore.

The defined speed ranges are determined by the speed flow curves and correspond with the optimal level of service (LoS) for traffic flow. Figure 5.6 shows the speed flow curve for expressways. If the average speed decreases (meaning more congestion), we increase the ERP rate; similarly, if it increases, we decrease the rate. We believe we have to be very clear about the rates and by how much and when they are adjusted.

- Rates are adjusted to keep traffic within optimal Level of Service (LoS)

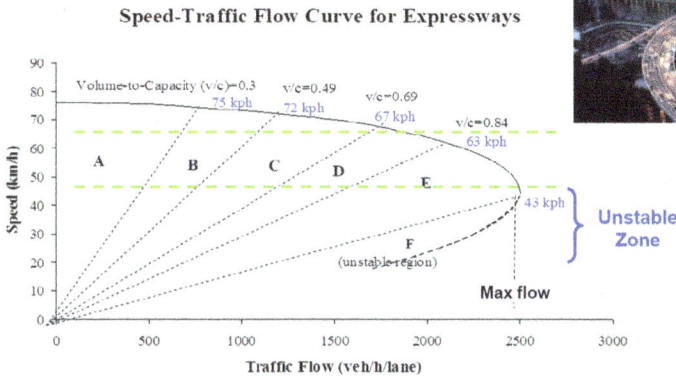

Figure 5.6 Determining speed ranges
Source: Local Transport Authority, Singapore.

In many ways, our ERP is fair, and we can monitor traffic conditions in terms of congestion measured by average speed and adjust our charging regime. During school holidays, for example, we remove the charges because there is no congestion, which people think is fair. So the integrity of the system works when drivers recognise that when and where roads are congested, they pay a charge, but when they are not congested, the charge is reduced or removed. We are considering extending the ERP to include charging by distance travelled, which will be more cost efficient for the city, and increasing charges for parking.

Since 1975, congestion has not increased in Singapore's CBD, despite significant increases in vehicle use. Figure 5.7 shows the effectiveness of congestion charging.

Index

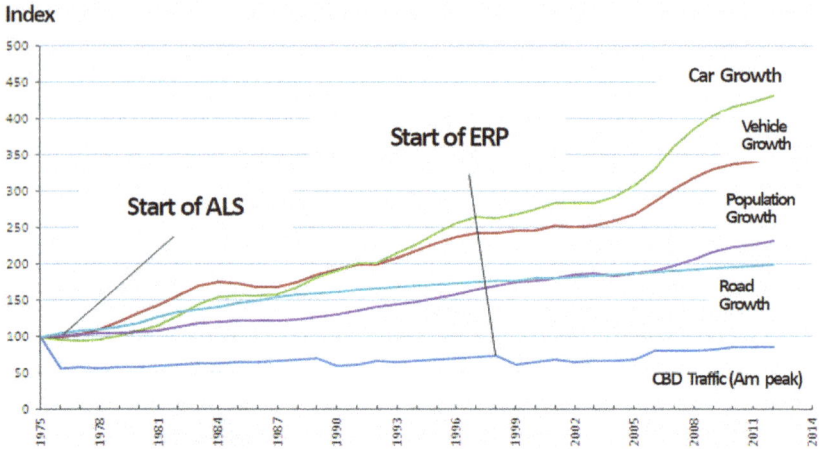

Figure 5.7 Effectiveness of Area Licensing Scheme and Electronic Road Pricing

Source: Local Transport Authority, Singapore.

Future mobility

In terms of future mobility in the city, we are planning for an era of 'smart mobility', including developing 'ERP2' with Global Navigation Satellite System (GNSS) technology to avoid building more gantries. We will introduce advanced big-data analytics, better demand management and an intelligent transport system as set out in our smart mobility vision for 2030.

In terms of autonomous vehicles (AVs), we are looking at four main issues: fixed and scheduled services, point-to-point mobility on demand, freight and utility. We believe that AV—appropriately applied to provide mobility solutions—can help to reduce demand for car ownership, reduce road congestion during peak hours and reduce reliance on human resources. We think we are in a good position to make this happen as we work promptly on the three key enablers: regulation, technology and public acceptance.

We cannot allow our city-state to become dysfunctional because of congestion—as so many global cities already are. Our vision is quite clear. We have four objectives. First, build more connectivity into the system. Second, provide better services that people want and use. Third, open the system to all, enabling us to enhance our liveability and maintain an inclusive community. And fourth, reduce the level of car ownership to minimise congestion. At the centre of our land transport management is government regulation—regulation that is strategic, has community acceptance and is supported by smart technology to produce better outcomes. Congestion is a cost we all suffer unless it is well managed and alternatives are attractive. We need to be focused on long-term planning, because it clearly sets out our future directions and allows us to manage accordingly. We believe in using economic transaction-based price signals to inform policy and manage the transport system. Our intent is to use market signals and incentives (or disincentives) to change behaviour to enable the optimal operating viability and best cost–benefit ratio for the community. That is how we work.

Section 3: Road pricing

6

Is pricing road transport significantly different to pricing other network infrastructure?

Alex Robson

Introduction

Australian governments have faced a number of challenges implementing significant policy reforms over the past few decades. The road transport sector is one area where reform has proved particularly challenging. Explaining the problems associated with road usage—especially in relation to funding issues, maintenance, road pricing and congestion charging—is not an easy task. In many areas, we already have user charging for the private enjoyment of publicly provided goods (for example, universities, utilities, rail transport and ports), but not generally in relation to roads, outside a few toll corridors and tunnels. Many argue that this situation will need to change to ensure a more efficient allocation of scarce resources and to align supply with demand.

Proponents of user charging argue that it is intended to serve two broad economic purposes. On the demand side, user charges are intended to provide a transparent price signal of the direct opportunity or resource costs of a project to those who derive direct benefits from its provision. The main idea behind such a price signal is that the introduction of a user charge will encourage efficient resource utilisation of a given facility—

in economic terms, up to the point where marginal benefits equal marginal resource costs. This price signal will have the effect of limiting the possibility that the facility will be over-utilised. The second objective relates to the supply side: appropriately designed user-charging arrangements may provide a signal to the private sector and the government, assisting them to allocate resources efficiently across a range of projects and other uses, so policy objectives can be achieved in a cost-effective manner.

Although price signals can in principle help to achieve these objectives, they are by no means a panacea. Across Australia, we currently have a range of indirect forms of road charging that raise funds, but which on the whole do not provide direct price signals for usage. For passenger vehicles, the main levy is the Commonwealth's fuel excise, which is estimated to amount to a tax of 5.5 cents per kilometre travelled by motorists. We also have other indirect user charges—such as myriad vehicle registration fees and motor vehicle stamp duties on new vehicles and transfers of ownership. Australia, therefore, currently has a *two-part cost recovery scheme* for road use involving both federal and state levels of government, with 'fixed' charges represented by vehicle registration requirements plus a 'marginal' charge through the fuel excise levy, which is tied to usage. One of the main problems today—and a principal concern for policymakers—is that the marginal charge does not always reflect social marginal costs. Many argue, for example, that charges are too low on congested roads and too high on uncongested roads.

Marginal cost and average cost pricing

Most of the economic issues associated with pricing are not new. Figure 6.1 shows an idealised example of an infrastructure project. Average costs (AC) of supply, which include fixed, upfront construction costs, tend to be higher than the marginal cost (MC).

In Figure 6.1, when marginal benefits (MB) (at the point Q*) equal marginal costs (MC), we have an efficient level of output (but note the exception discussed below). The problem is that if the facility has fixed costs (AC), the public (or private) entity that is going to run such facilities will run at a loss under marginal cost pricing, since average costs exceed marginal costs. The rectangle between D–AC–MC represents the fact that this entity is running at a loss, and that loss has to be subsidised from somewhere. This is a well-known, fundamental issue with marginal cost pricing: even though it generally could be implemented, it is not necessarily 'incentive compatible' in that it will not align usage with average costs or allow the owner to break even.

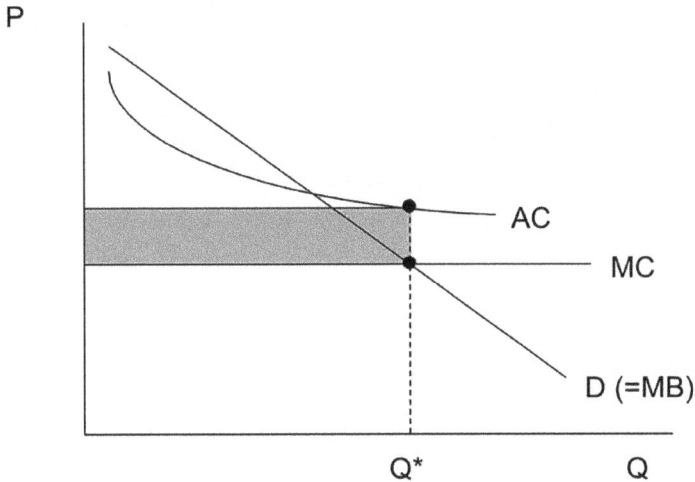

Figure 6.1 Marginal cost pricing
Source: Author's work.

Another issue in relation to marginal cost pricing is the argument put forward by Ronald Coase (1946). Suppose that government provides a good or service and commits to price it at a marginal cost. If fixed costs are high—so that average costs remain high—then under the marginal cost pricing rule we could achieve some 'optimal' level of usage at Q*. At this point, marginal benefits appear to equal marginal costs, but what could in fact occur is that the project is socially wasteful (see Figure 6.2). The reason is the fixed costs are just too high. So, in this situation, it is straightforward to design an infrastructure pricing scheme for which the price equals marginal costs, but this is a project that should not go ahead at all. In summary, we can get people to reveal their demand curve by having some sort of pricing scheme where price equals the marginal cost, but that does not necessarily have anything to do with whether the project is a good idea in the first place. In cases like this, Coase proposed the idea of a two-part tariff, with an access fee to cover fixed costs and a price per unit equal to marginal costs.

Price

AC(Q*)

Average Cost

Marginal Cost

Demand (=MB)

Q*

Quantity

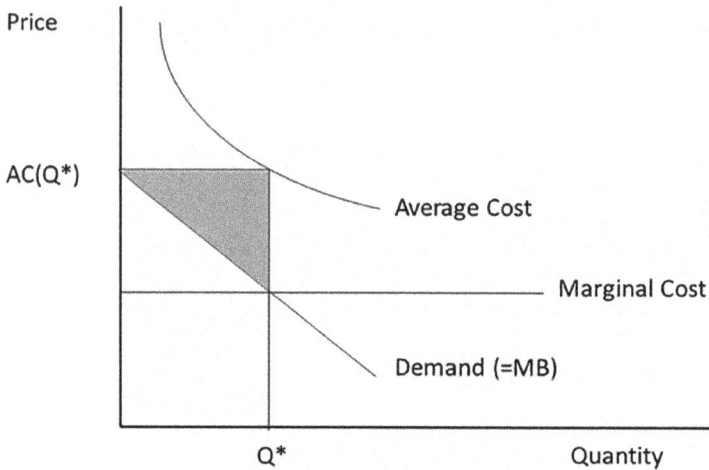

Figure 6.2 Marginal cost pricing may produce a socially wasteful outcome
Source: Author's work.

Another alternative is average cost pricing (see Figure 6.3). The issue here is that we immediately get an efficiency loss: the project breaks even, but there is a deadweight loss triangle because price exceeds marginal cost. This is a second-best outcome. We may be willing to put up with that, but it is not a first-best solution.

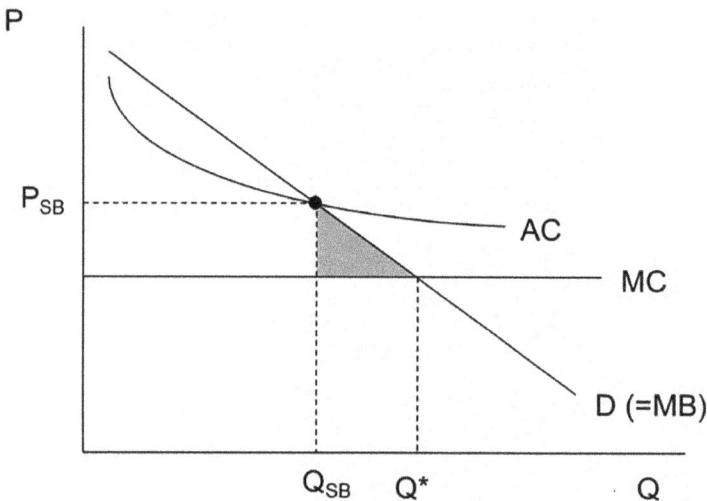

P

P_{SB}

AC

MC

D (=MB)

Q_{SB} Q*

Q

Figure 6.3 Average cost pricing
Source: Author's work.

A practical issue with average cost pricing concerns implementation. If the average cost curve cuts the demand curve at two or more points, we have to decide which average cost will actually be charged. Figure 6.4 shows this situation. At the point (P_0, Q_0), price equals average cost, so the project breaks even. But this is not a second-best point, because the deadweight loss is higher than it would be at the other point in the diagram where the average cost curve cuts the demand curve. So an average cost pricing rule provides only a partial answer in this situation.

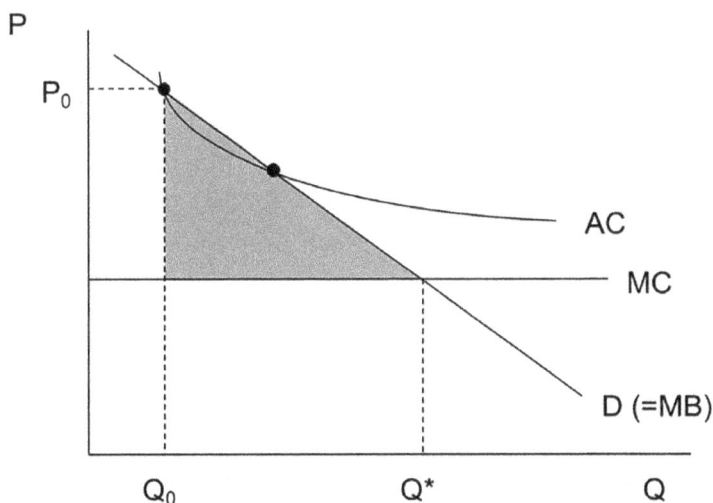

Figure 6.4 Average cost pricing: Which average cost?
Source: Author's work.

A final difficulty with average cost pricing is that it may not even be feasible—in the following sense. In Figure 6.5, the area under the demand curve far outweighs the total cost of the project, so this is a project that is socially beneficial. But there is no average cost price that exists here that will allow the project to break even. The basic lesson is that, although these pricing rules—marginal cost and average cost pricing—are simple in theory, they are likely to face a range of difficulties in practice.

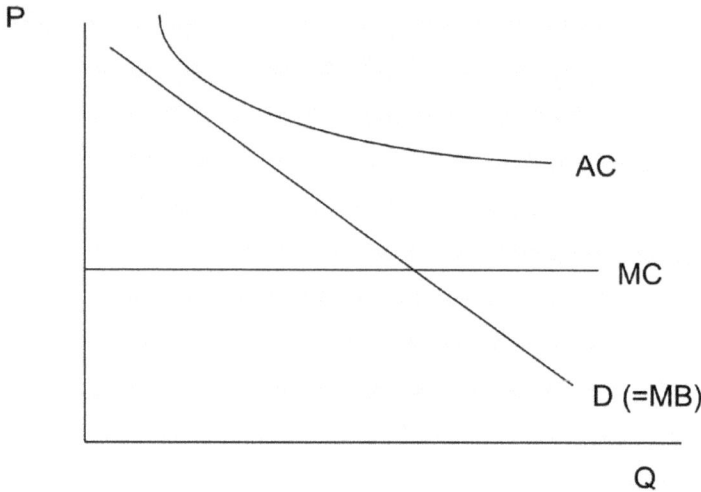

Figure 6.5 Average cost pricing: Existence?
Source: Author's work.

Congestion pricing

Policymakers often face a range of other issues in relation to road users. One well-known issue is the concentrated times that consumers use the infrastructure. This raises issues around congestion pricing. When there is high road use, a road becomes an example of an 'open access' or 'common pool' resource: it is non-excludable, but rival in consumption. Congestion is a classic example of a 'negative externality', and we get non-price rationing in the form of queuing and long delays. This likely represents an efficiency loss, as some people with higher-value uses face delays and the social cost of lost time, and the congestion may have even completely excluded some high-value users.

The idea of congestion pricing is that it tries to produce a better allocation of that road space to high-value users. Roads with high-value users can gain, but those with low value can potentially lose. Figure 6.6 illustrates a situation in which we have a classic example of a congestion externality: at the margin, social costs exceed private costs. The optimal outcome here is to set a Pigouvian tax or charge that reflects the 'negative externality' at the optimum, which is at Q* in Figure 6.6. In the absence of a charge, we get a welfare loss of G, which is the sum of the excess of social costs at the margin over social benefits at the margin from driving.

Optimal congestion pricing operates as follows. At point Q^{**}, social marginal benefits equal social marginal costs. The optimal charge is the gap between marginal benefits and costs at this point, and is indicated on the vertical axis on the left-hand side of the figure. When this charge is introduced, there are some people who will be 'tolled off' (lying between Q^* and Q^{**}), and they will choose to no longer drive, reducing overall demand. Naturally, they are personally going to lose out, as shown in area F—the excess of their private benefits over the costs they faced before the charge was introduced.

On the other hand, road users who continue to use the road will have quicker commute times, because now their costs of travelling are lower by C plus D. But notice that their travel cost, plus the monetary cost (A plus B), is actually higher than the total travel costs they initially faced.

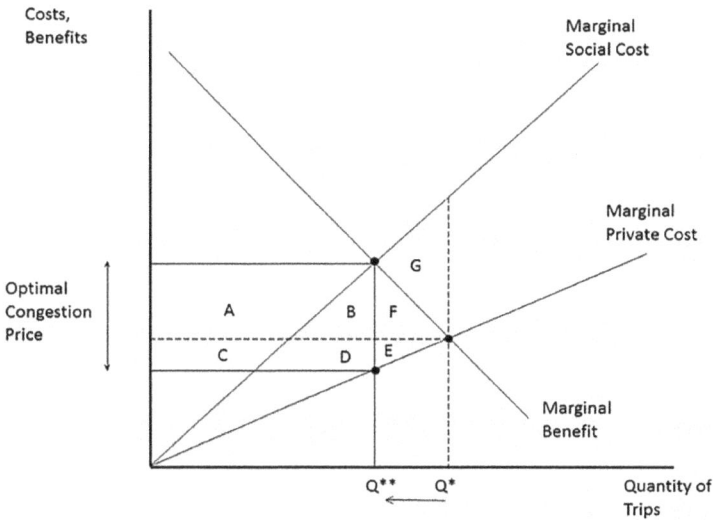

Figure 6.6 Congestion pricing
Source: Author's work.

This brings us to one of the major potential problems with congestion road pricing—and one that could explain why it has not taken off in Australia: at the optimal charge, people who continue to drive will be worse off. They save on their travel time, but the optimal charge increases their overall costs of travel. Society as a whole gains, because the government gains revenue from the toll. The net social gain is G (we have eliminated the original deadweight loss). Equivalently, the net gain is C plus D minus F, which is equivalent to the area G.

In summary, the issue governments face is that drivers who are going to be tolled will in fact face a charge that—from an individually rational point of view—they do not want to pay. Simply put, when we levy the optimal toll, people are going to feel it in their hip pocket and will feel directly worse off—even though there is less congestion. So, although cultural or historical factors may be important for explaining why tolls have been unpopular in Australia, economics provides us with an alternative explanation: drivers may be worse off, even though congestion falls and society as a whole is better off.

This suggests that while it is always possible to think in the abstract about an efficient congestion pricing regime, implementing such a charge is going to be very difficult politically. Governments would need to persuade people that this is a good idea, either by using the revenue wisely or by carefully hypothecating it and using it as a sort of persuasive device (which may have its own efficiency costs).

Other practical difficulties with congestion pricing

Measuring benefits

There is a range of other practical difficulties that governments face if they are trying to convince people that congestion pricing is a good idea. In assessing any congestion pricing scheme, it is important to take care that we are counting benefits properly. Measurements of the *total* costs of congestion abound, but from an economic point of view they are not particularly interesting. What should ultimately be of interest to policymakers are the congestion costs that are avoided if an optimal pricing scheme is implemented. Some amount of congestion is efficient; it would not be optimal to have no congestion at all. The upper bound of the net benefit of congestion charging is the area G in Figure 6.6 (and it really is an upper bound, because congestion pricing schemes can be costly to run). Importantly, notwithstanding the total costs of congestion, if a significant portion of the revenue from congestion pricing is spent on collection costs, or is wasted, this could outweigh the benefits, G, and the pricing scheme could actually make society worse off.

On the other hand, there are other benefits to consider. In addition to savings in journey times for commuters, there are reductions in fuel use and pollution emissions. Accident externalities and their associated costs may also fall, although this is by no means certain; a reduction in congestion may induce commuters to drive faster. In the long run, society may also benefit from a better allocation of road space.

Spillover effects

Another well-known difficulty is the potential for charging on one road to have spillover effects on to untolled roads. Introducing a charge on one road may simply divert traffic and worsen congestion on other roads. Any real-world assessment of congestion pricing ought to account for these costs as well.

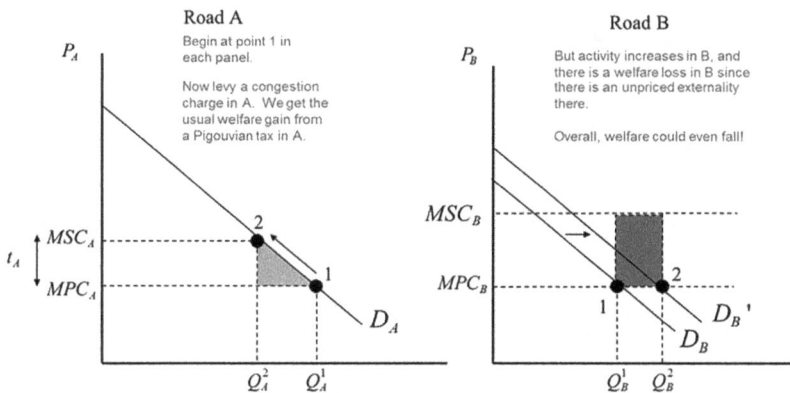

Figure 6.7 Example 1: Incomplete congestion charging
Source: Author's work.

Figure 6.7 illustrates the theory, but there are many examples of this in practical policymaking. Alcohol taxation—specifically, the recent 'alcopops tax' (introduced in 2008)—is a good case in point. The alcopops tax was supposedly designed as a kind of Pigouvian tax on certain types of alcoholic beverages. The practical problem was that it was easy to substitute alcopops for other types of alcoholic beverages with their own social costs. If those costs have not been priced correctly, there will be a negative welfare effect from switching to those other things that could outweigh the positive effect of reduced alcopop consumption. The same phenomenon is possible with higher tobacco taxation, where the effect of reducing tobacco use might be that consumers switch to other socially undesirable things (such as hard drugs or other illegal substances), which themselves are not taxed in the optimum Pigouvian way.

Other examples abound. With congestion pricing, the concern is that while we may be able to reduce congestion on one road, this may lead to people doing 'rat runs'—using other roads—and simply shifting the congestion into other areas. This then reduces the welfare gains identified in Figure 6.5, and we could end up with a negative overall welfare effect if these other distortions are large enough.

Another possible difficulty with congestion charges is that, while there will be fewer people choosing to drive, they may not have alternative modes of transport (such as convenient, easily accessible, inexpensive public transport). In response to a congestion charge, individuals may decide to not work at all. This would reduce labour supply, which is already distorted by other taxes such as income taxes, payroll taxes and the goods and services tax (GST). So there could be a welfare loss in the labour market that needs to be accounted for (see Figure 6.8).

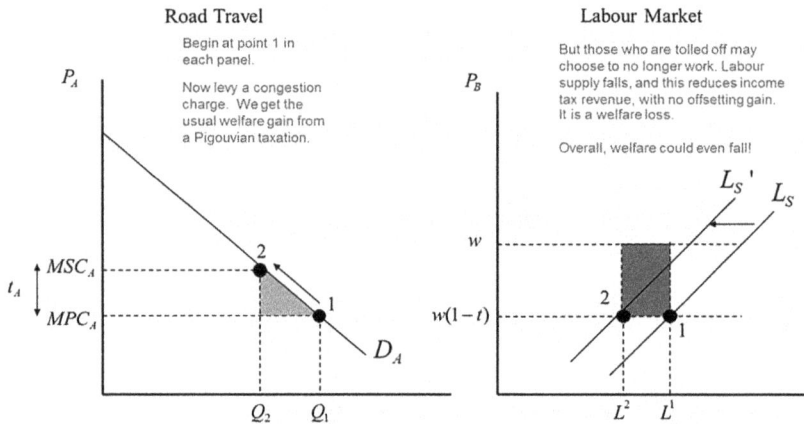

Figure 6.8 Example 2: Interaction with labour taxes
Source: Author's work.

These spillover effects may seem like esoteric points, but in the real world they are very important. The essential point is that we are likely to produce unwanted spillover effects in markets that are already distorted and, if these effects are large enough, we need to count them in any cost–benefit analysis of road pricing.

Forecasting demand

Another practical difficulty in regards to road pricing in Australia is forecasting performance. The simple models examined above assumed that policymakers knew what traffic demand looked like and how it would respond to the introduction of a toll. If the traffic forecast turns out to be wrong, additional costs can ensue. Suppose, for example, that the government has implemented a toll in such a way as to balance out expected marginal benefits and expected marginal costs. Figure 6.9 shows what that toll might look like. If, however, actual demand turns out to be lower than expected, from an efficiency point of view, the imposed toll should have been lower. In Figure 6.9, the toll is far too high, producing a social loss because the traffic forecast was wrong.

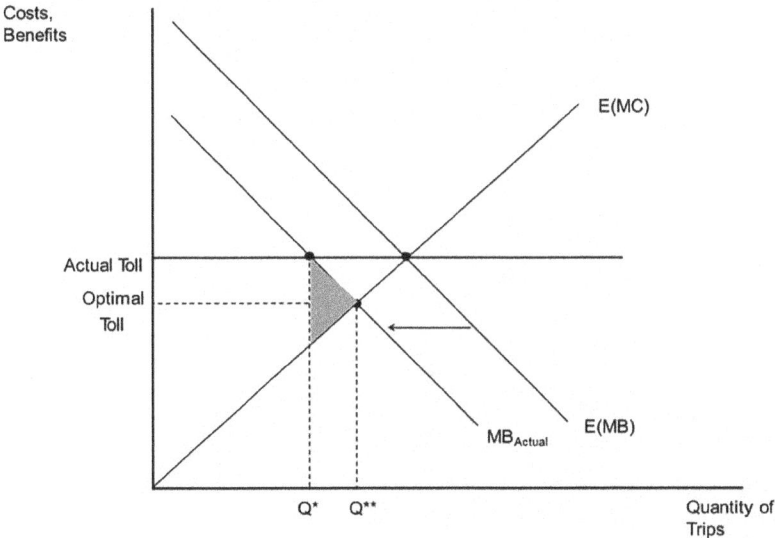

Figure 6.9 Social costs of poor traffic demand forecasting performance
Source: Author's work.

This has been a genuine problem in Australia. Table 6.1, which was put together by Robert Bianchi at Griffith University, shows the performance of toll roads in Australia over the past decade or so. In most cases, it has not been good. Li and Hensher (2010) point out that demand forecast errors in Australia have, on average, been minus 45 per cent—actual demand tends to be 45 per cent lower than predicted. The cost of over-forecasting demand is one that must be taken into account when we are thinking about the benefits and costs of various policies.

Table 6.1 Average toll road traffic performance since 2000

Australian Toll Road Traffic Performance: Openings Since 2000				
Project	City	Opened	Actual Traffic vs Forecast	Comments
CityLink	Melbourne	Dec 2000	+10%	• Road took 7 years to reach forecasts.
Cross City Tunnel	Sydney	Aug 2005	-56%	• Receivers appointed in December 2006. • Sold to ABN AMRO/Leighton for $700m in June 2007 (cost $1bn)
Westlink M7	Sydney	Dec 2005	-40%	• Road underperformed in terms of trips, but compensated in terms of trip distance.
Lane Cove Tunnel	Sydney	Mar 2007	-60%	• Receiver appointed in January 2010. • Sold to Transurban for $630m in May 2010 (cost $1.1bn). • $160m legal action launched against traffic forecasters in September 2009.
EastLink	Melbourne	Jun 2008	-39%	• Shares slumped from $1 to 45 cents. • Delisted and sold to CP2 for $2.2bn in October 2011 (cost $2.5bn).
CLEM7	Brisbane	Mar 2010	-76%	• Cost $3bn with $700m equity and $1.3bn debt • Shares are worth $0. • Receivers appointed in February 2011. • $150m class action lawsuit lagainst traffic forecasters in May 2012. • $2bn legal action launched against traffic forecasters by receivers in May 2012.
New Gateway Bridge	Brisbane	May 2010	n/a	n/a
Go Between Bridge	Brisbane	Jul 2010	-49%	• Toll tariffs have been 25%-45% below anticipated levels, so revenue underperformance exceeds traffic underperformance.
Airport Link	Brisbane	Jul 2012	-45%	• Road has been operating toll-free. • Underperformance prompts operator to revise toll introduction, now with (unanticipated) discounted rates for the first 6 months.
			Average = -44%	

Source: Robert Bianchi.

Congestion charging as monopoly pricing

Another issue that could arise in practice is if congestion charging is used purely as a revenue-raising device. Governments are often in positions where they are pure monopoly providers of roads and can therefore charge a price (or allow a private provider to charge a price) that maximises profits, rather than the optimal congestion charge. In Figure 6.10, the price charged is relatively high, but the welfare loss caused by the monopoly pricing here is shown in the shaded area to the left. The welfare gain that could have been obtained is the shaded area to the right. It is not clear which of those triangles is larger here; if governments are going to use road pricing just as a revenue-raising device and act like a pure monopoly, they could end up making things worse.

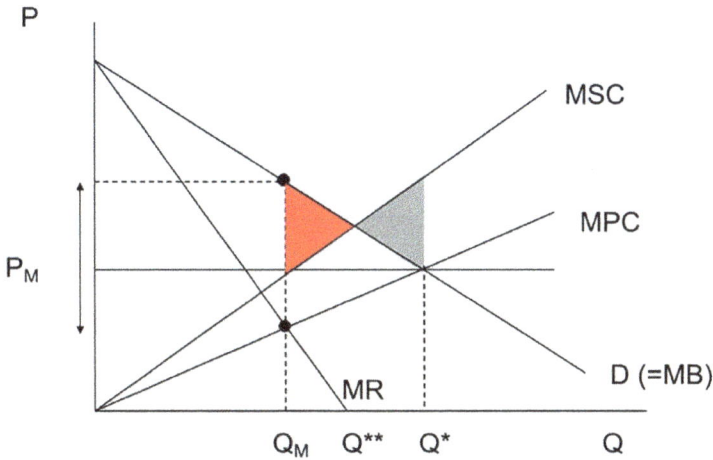

Figure 6.10 Congestion charging as a pure revenue-raising device
Source: Author's work.

Conclusion: The importance of rigorous cost–benefit analysis

All of this points to the need for careful cost–benefit analysis of pricing schemes and road charges, because it is by no means a foregone conclusion that pricing is always going to provide net benefits. As this chapter has demonstrated, in theory, we can think of cases where pricing schemes are a good idea, but it is just as easy to think of cases where they are not.

One of the main reasons for undertaking a rigorous cost–benefit analysis is to reduce or eliminate theoretical ambiguities and deal with two types of errors:

- There is a policy that is beneficial, but is not adopted because the initial assessment is that it is not beneficial—and no cost–benefit analysis is conducted to demonstrate that the initial perception is incorrect.
- A bad project goes ahead (but would not have proceeded if a cost–benefit analysis had been undertaken).

A good cost–benefit analysis will not always give the perfect answer or completely eliminate uncertainties, but it will tend to reduce the probabilities of making these kinds of policy errors.

I conclude with a word of caution from a well-known infrastructure example that illustrates what can happen in public policy when policymakers do not use cost–benefit analyses appropriately: the National Broadband Network. No cost–benefit analysis of the initial rollout of fibre-optic cable was undertaken, and costs and timing have subsequently blown out. Ergas and Robson (2009) undertook such an analysis and found that the project's costs would exceed its benefits by somewhere between $40 billion and $20 billion, depending on the discount rate used. A proper cost–benefit analysis would have identified many of the subsequent construction and cost risks.

References

Coase, R. H. (1946). The marginal cost controversy. *Economica* 13(51): 169–82.

Ergas, H. and Robson, A. R. W. (2009). The social losses from inefficient infrastructure projects: Recent Australian experience. 17–18 August. Available from: www.academia.edu/8569365/THE_SOCIAL_LOSSES_ FROM_INEFFICIENT_INFRASTRUCTURE_PROJECTS_RECENT_ AUSTRALIAN_EXPERIENCE

Li, Z. and Hensher, D. A. (2010). Toll roads in Australia: An overview of characteristics and accuracy of demand forecasts. *Transport Reviews* 30(5): 541–69. doi.org/10.1080/01441640903211173

7

Using road pricing as a viable option to meet Australia's future road funding needs

Brendan Lyon

Australia faces two problems in road transportation: on the supply side, we face diminishing revenues to maintain and expand the road network; and, on the demand side, we lack any effective tools to manage congestion or shape peak demand periods.

Together, these factors see lower capital, productive and allocative efficiency in road transport—hence our rapidly escalating economic and social costs. Various reports by the Productivity Commission, the Bureau of Infrastructure, Transport and Regional Economics (BITRE), Infrastructure Australia, Infrastructure Partnerships Australia and others outline these challenges.

In this chapter, I will discuss where we can act to address these essential transport challenges, what this might mean for the road network and users and what it (ideally) means for those who are working in policy roles with the government—and why you should be enthusiastic and actively involved in this issue.

Everything old is new again

User charges through both public tolls and even identifiable early forerunners of modern road public–private partnerships (PPPs) have been used from the earliest days of colonial Australia.

The first toll way, a bridge, opened in 1802, just 14 years after the First Fleet made landfall and almost a century before Federation (New South Wales Parliament Legislative Council 2017). Indeed, by the later nineteenth century, colonial Sydney had numerous tolling plazas, with tolls levied to fund the expansion and maintenance of the road network.

Modern road PPPs also have recognisable precedent in colonial times. The original Pyrmont Bridge in Sydney is one such example. Opening in 1858, the bridge was privately developed and financed, with colonial legislation granting a right to the owners to levy a differential toll on users—essentially the same as a modern PPP.

This relatively long history of tolls and charges involved community issues similar to those in modern times. Figure 7.1 is an excerpt from an 1863 letter to the *Sydney Morning Herald* by Mr John Pendrill, complaining about aspects of the Pyrmont Bridge charge. I note that Mr Pendrill continued to use the bridge—because it was convenient.

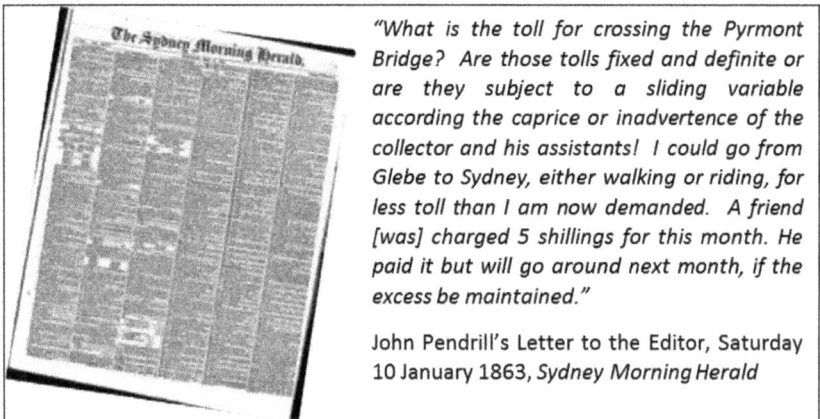

"What is the toll for crossing the Pyrmont Bridge? Are those tolls fixed and definite or are they subject to a sliding variable according the caprice or inadvertence of the collector and his assistants! I could go from Glebe to Sydney, either walking or riding, for less toll than I am now demanded. A friend [was] charged 5 shillings for this month. He paid it but will go around next month, if the excess be maintained."

John Pendrill's Letter to the Editor, Saturday 10 January 1863, *Sydney Morning Herald*

Figure 7.1 Variable tolling in 1863
Source: *Sydney Morning Herald*, 10 January 1863.

Pendrill's letter reflects two points that remain true today. First, while people will never love paying for access, they will pay where it provides value. This relates to Alex Robson's point (Chapter 6, this volume) about choosing the right assets, with the right capacity and in the right places. The second point is that opposition to user charging is not new; it has always been and remains a sharp aspect of the infrastructure debate.

From road tolls to road pricing

Beyond individual 'facility' tollways, a wider concept of whole-network road user models has a much shorter history. The Industry Commission (now Productivity Commission) developed road pricing concepts in its *Rail Transport* report (Industry Commission 1991).

While that report principally considered the operational structure of public sector railways, it also developed a case for rationalised, cost-reflective transport pricing across the wider transport network, across modes and across different journey types. This work shows the very high level of policy sophistication in the Industry Commission at that time, given that enabling technologies such as the Global Positioning System (GPS) and even free-flow tolling based on radio-frequency identification (RFID) were yet to come into existence.

Revenue decay creates a burning platform for change

Our analysis of contemporary transport infrastructure funding sources showed substantial decay in the Commonwealth fuel excise, with the earlier de-indexation of the fuel tax and a consumer shift towards fuel-efficient vehicles combining to halve federal fuel excise revenues as a proportion of receipts.

Infrastructure Partnerships Australia released its first volume of work on the structure of Australia's road transport market in early 2010, reflecting our view that structural change in some form was unavoidable because of this debased revenue model. Reflecting the Industry Commission's (much) earlier work, our paper developed concepts for a system where the road-related taxes and charges become a fundamental response to improve the productive, allocative and dynamic efficiency challenges affecting Australia's transport system.

Ultimately, our paper resolved the abolition of the current federal/state 'fuel tax plus rego' two-part tariff in favour of a much more sophisticated and equitable pricing model, with charges calculated on:

- the distance travelled
- vehicle mass
- the location of use
- the time of day.

This is an economically efficient but radically different model to what we are used to—a pricing model that allows costs of use, including congestion, to be made explicit to the user rather than absorbed by the community at large.

Road pricing and funding reform principles

Noting the potential for (sometimes extreme) community and political sensitivity to major reform options, we released our 2010 paper to develop key concepts, but also to provide a basis for discussion of the issue with policymakers and, particularly, with the major motoring clubs.

This was deliberate because, practically, road pricing would be unlikely to receive any degree of policy consideration if the key user groups opposed it.

In what is an enduring credit to Australia's motoring clubs, far from being opposed to change, they were highly engaged and highly knowledgeable. Brian Negus from the Royal Automobile Club of Victoria (RACV) and then CEO of the Australian Automobile Association (AAA) Andrew McKellar deserve particular credit for their willingness to engage and to lead on this issue—as does Michael Bradley, the current AAA CEO.

By 2014, our partnership with the motoring clubs saw us jointly release a major study called *Road Pricing and Transport Infrastructure Funding: Reform pathways for Australia* (Infrastructure Partnerships Australia 2014). It is available on the Infrastructure Partnerships Australia website and is an interesting piece of work.

This paper addressed important questions, particularly around how rationalised pricing might affect typical users—for example, people in regional areas.

In this way, it allowed the motoring clubs to adopt a position on this difficult issue—and, in so doing, to signal to policymakers they were up for a process of serious structural change.

While we have not published on this yet, the revenue hypothecation aspect of our reformed pricing model should be supported by complementary measures to enhance the dynamic efficiency of road transport, through adopting utility-type regulation of capital investments and operating expenditures. This could inform user price setting, but also simultaneously take road transport legitimately 'off budget' and remove it from political or geographic bias in capital expenditures.

The four fundamental problems in Australia's contemporary road transport sector

Our 2014 paper identified four fundamental problems:

1. The revenue model is fundamentally debased.
2. There is an opaque connection between revenue collection and network investment.
3. There is a lack of sophistication in the two-part tariff pricing model (as also noted by Alex Robson in this volume).
4. The current pricing model sees inequitable outcomes for user groups.

We resolved that, for these fundamental reasons, the current system is not sustainable in the longer term without change.

The terminal revenue model

Figure 7.2 shows the terminal decay of the Commonwealth fuel excise, which, by 2010–11, had almost halved in proportional terms. This has been led by two factors. First, the biannual indexation of fuel excise to the consumer price index (CPI) was abolished in 2001 and not reintroduced until 2014–15. The second, continuing and now accelerating factor is the community's shift to fuel-efficient, hybrid and 'fuel-free' electric vehicles.

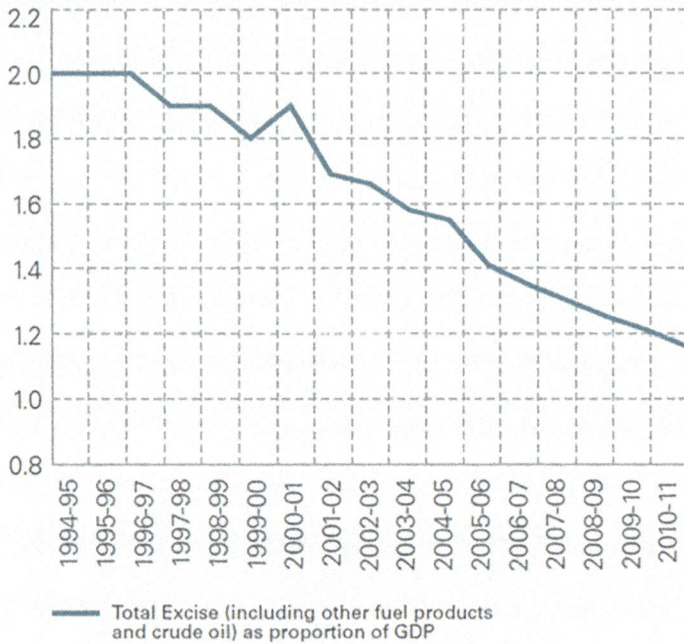

Figure 7.2 Fuel excise as a proportion of gross domestic product (GDP)
Source: Infrastructure Partnerships Australia (2014).

It's opaque

A key benefit of structural change is the opportunity to fundamentally connect what users are charged with what funds are expended—and on what. The current system has developed organically over a century or so, with predictably confused structures and a resulting lack of transparency and accountability. Figure 7.3 describes the status quo.

A key aspect of our model is the hypothecation of road-related taxes and charges to transport—thereby insulating motorists from subsidising consolidated revenue—and insulating state treasuries from subsidising motorists.

Hypothecation would allow the revenue collection envelope to be calculated, based on determination of allowed levels of capital investment, and transparency and review of the cost to motorists from the operation and maintenance of the wider road network.

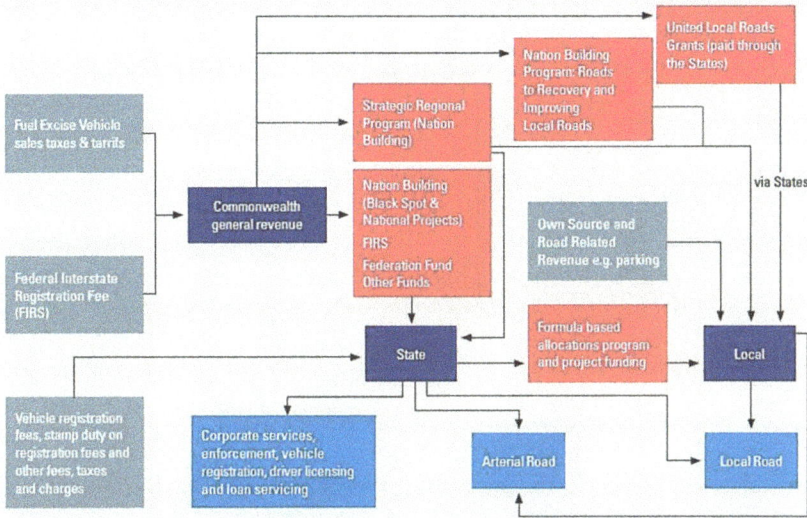

Figure 7.3 There is no link between revenue and investment
Source: Infrastructure Partnerships Australia (2014).

It's unsophisticated

While the fuel excise was designed to price road consumption, it cannot make fuel consumed in peak hour in Melbourne or Sydney more expensive than fuel consumed on, for example, a regional road. This means the road pricing model lacks the sophistication to manage urban congestion—the most obvious, the most frustrating and the most costly transport challenge.

Australia's road network is available 24 hours a day; it endures excessive demand during the relatively short commuter and weekend peaks in major cities, but it also sees massive underutilisation during other periods, particularly overnight. There is a practical limit to the number of new lanes that can be built on motorways, meaning that some form of demand management will be needed in key areas.

Congestion could be resolved through the type of cordon or area charging schemes considered and assessed in our paper (and discussed by Alex Robson in Chapter 6); but in our work we found that this would neglect the important opportunities to increase the overall performance of road transport.

The Productivity Commission has recently produced two reports on the pricing and funding of roads that attempted to resolve such important transport issues. The first report, chaired by Gary Banks in 2006, attempted to calculate the actual costs of road and rail freight infrastructure, with a view to introducing user charging for heavy road usage. It also attempted to calculate the costs of congestion. The second report, in 2015, chaired by Peter Harris, looked more broadly at user charging and optimal models for road funding and reflects the concepts in Infrastructure Partnerships Australia's work on the topic. This second report contained two important recommendations (DIRD 2014: 11):

Recommendation 8.1

The first step in a long-term transition to a more efficient and effective approach to the provision and funding of roads should be the establishment of Road Funds by State and Territory Governments. State Governments, and local government associations, should actively encourage and support local governments to form regional Road Funds for networks of local roads. To be effective, Road Funds should:

- have the objective of clearly linking road-user preferences with investment and maintenance decisions
- integrate the tasks of road funding and provision
- have a significant degree of autonomy
- have access to adequate revenue to meet the costs of the road network they administer, as required by the relevant road users
- entail transparent processes for determining the level and allocation of funds
- include an open and transparent procedure for direct involvement of road users and consultation with the broader community on project selection, funding, and road charging decisions
- involve systematic post-project evaluation and periodic review of the arrangements.

The implementation of Road Funds should take into account the research and analysis developed for heavy vehicles by the Heavy Vehicle Charging and Investment reform project ...

Recommendation 4.1

The Australian Government should actively encourage State and Territory Governments to undertake pilot studies on how vehicle telematics could be used for distance and location charging of cars and other light vehicles. To do so, the Australian Government should:

- offer to partly fund these pilot studies
- work with the States and Territories to address privacy concerns and share lessons from the trials and overseas experience
- ensure that motorists are directly involved via roads and motorists associations.

The pilot studies should be designed to inform future consideration of a shift to direct road user charging for cars and other light vehicles, with the revenue hypothecated to roads. Heavy vehicle trials could also be developed on a similar basis. The Road Funds proposed in recommendation 8.1 could be tasked to undertake the trials if this does not result in unreasonable delay.

What are we trying to achieve?

Across policy work, Infrastructure Partnerships Australia emphasises the need to identify the fundamental outcomes sought through change.

In our 2014 paper on road pricing, we refined these 'first principles' into a simple assessment framework through which to analyse the spectrum of potential pricing models. We filtered these models against their ability to deliver:

- adequate revenue to sustainably fund transport network expansions such as new roads
- adequate revenue to fund appropriate maintenance
- a fairer allocation of costs and benefits in the transport market
- funding stream security
- improved network performance.

It's nice to have options

Cordon or area charging was the first model we assessed. The community is broadly familiar with these types of schemes, which operate, for example, in London, Stockholm, Milan and Singapore. Our assessment showed that while these are relatively simple to design and implement and observably effective in dealing with congestion, there are limitations to simply bolting on additional charges in particular areas.

Table 7.1 Cordon area pricing assessment

CAN CORDON/AREA PRICING	CORDON/AREA PRICING
Fund additions to the transport network	✔
Fund network maintenance	🟡
Provide a fair allocation of costs and benefits	✔ 🟡
Provide a secure funding stream	✔
Provide the opportunity to improve network performance	🟡

🟡 = partially.

Source: Infrastructure Partnerships Australia (2014).

Next, we assessed a 'national highway improvement charge', a facility charge that would see revenue collected from, and reinvested in, particular roads, corridors or networks. This approach could allow the cost of particular roads or networks to be removed from government budgets—similar to some European networks such as Italy's Autostrada. As with cordon charging, this type of approach was found to be too limited when compared with the breadth of challenges facing Australian transport.

Table 7.2 Highway improvement charge assessment

CAN A NATIONAL HIGHWAY IMPROVEMENT CHARGE	NATIONAL HIGHWAY IMPROVEMENT CHARGE
Fund additions to the transport network	🟡
Fund network maintenance	✔
Provide a fair allocation of costs and benefits	✔ 🟡
Provide a secure funding stream	✔ 🟡
Provide the opportunity to improve network performance	✘

🟡 = partially.

Source: Infrastructure Partnerships Australia (2014).

Having rejected limited pricing models applying to all vehicles, but only on parts of the network, we next assessed a model that would apply to the whole network—but only to particular vehicles, such as freight vehicles. This kind of 'whole of network, partial fleet' pricing model offers substantial benefits in terms of a detailed trial for a broader road pricing reform, and could conceivably be progressively rolled out to cover additional vehicle classes. Logically, however, the full benefits of the pricing signals offered by a whole-of-network model would not be realised when only particular vehicles are covered, so the scheme only partially meets most of the objectives laid out for road pricing reform (see Table 7.3).

Table 7.3 Network pricing assessment

CAN THE SELECTED VEHICLE CLASS(ES), WHOLE-OF-NETWORK REGIME	SELECTED VEHICLE CLASS(ES), WHOLE-OF-NETWORK
Fund additions to the transport network	🟡
Fund network maintenance	🟡
Provide a fair allocation of costs and benefits	🟡
Provide a secure funding stream	✔ 🟡
Provide the opportunity to improve network performance	🟡 ✖

🟡 = partially.

Source: Infrastructure Partnerships Australia (2014).

Logically, given the scale of misallocations, inefficiencies, cross-subsidies and revenue decay in road transport, we found that enduring solutions could only be found through fundamental, systemic change.

Our universal road user charging (URUC) model would cover all vehicles and the entire road network and see the existing 'fuel tax plus rego' charges abolished, replaced with on-vehicle charging based on the time, mass, distance and location of use.

As shown in Table 7.4, our URUC delivered the broadest range of benefits, but would represent the deepest and widest microeconomic reform in several decades—no mean feat in today's policy environment!

Table 7.4 Assessment of universal road user charging model

CAN UNIVERSAL ROAD USER CHARGING	UNIVERSAL ROAD USER CHARGING (ALL VEHICLES, WHOLE NETWORK)
Fund additions to the transport network	✔
Fund network maintenance	✔
Provide a fair allocation of costs and benefits	✔
Provide a secure funding stream	✔
Provide the opportunity to improve network performance	✔

Source: Infrastructure Partnerships Australia (2014).

Table 7.5 shows the simplified options analysis, with the existing framework of road user charging used as the base case for assessment.

Table 7.5 Comparison of options

CHARGING REGIME / 'Problem to solve'	EXISTING FRAMEWORK	CORDON/AREA PRICING	NATIONAL HIGHWAY IMPROVEMENT CHARGE	SELECTED VEHICLE CLASS(ES), PARTIAL NETWORK	SELECTED VEHICLE CLASS(ES), WHOLE-OF-NETWORK	UNIVERSAL ROAD USER CHARGE (ALL VEHICLES, WHOLE NETWORK)
Funding additions to the transport network – can the charging regime provide a sustainable funding mechanism to provide capacity enhancements to the transport network?	red	green	yellow	yellow	yellow	green
Funding network maintenance – can the charging regime provide a secure and reactive funding source for network maintenance?	red	yellow	yellow	red + yellow	yellow	green
A fair allocation of costs and benefits – can the charging regime ensure a fair distribution of costs between users, where those who use more, pay more and those who use less, pay less?	red + yellow	yellow	green + green	yellow	yellow	green
Funding stream security – can the charging regime offer a secure funding stream that reflects changing demand for road usage and promotes longer term investment planning?	red	green + green	green + yellow	yellow + red	green + green	green
Improving network performance – can the charging regime provide appropriate pricing signals for road users and road providers to improve the performance of the network?	red	yellow	red	yellow	red + yellow	green

● = partially.

Source: Infrastructure Partnerships Australia (2014).

Impacts on users

To allow a thorough assessment of the typical user price impacts that might be expected under the proposed URUC, we defined a number of 'test users'. The rationale for generating test users was to provide a sample of different types of light vehicle to compare and contrast the different components of the model and provide 'real-world' user comparisons against the existing charging regime. These test users are shown in Figure 7.4.

USER	AGE	LOCATION	TRAVELLING CHARACTERISTICS
1. Peter	62	Victoria, Regional City	• Owns one car – 2009 Holden Cruze (Vehicle 1) • Owns one light commercial vehicle – 2005 Toyota HiAce (Vehicle 2) • Operates own furniture restoration business, is required to use van for pick up and deliveries • At least once a week, travels on national highway network to make deliveries • Uses car three to four times per week for personal use, travelling only short distances
2. Graham	45	NSW, Sydney, outer suburbs	• Family owns 2 cars – 2009 Audi A4 (Vehicle 1) and Jeep Grand Cherokee (Vehicle 2) • Graham drives to work every day and parks at office (Audi), drives on motorways (one way journey length 26 km) • His wife uses 2010 Jeep Grand Cherokee to short distances in local area (e.g. school drop off and pick up, other personal business) • Frequent weekend usage (both vehicles)
3. Leanne	32	South East Queensland, outer urban area	• Owns one car – 2007 Toyota Corolla (Vehicle 1) • Night shift worker, travels to work (cross city, non-CBD) in the early evening and returns home before the AM peak period • Occasional weekend usage, generally travelling short distances in local area

Figure 7.4 Avatars representing different road user profiles
Source: Infrastructure Partnerships Australia (2014).

Peter, the first avatar, owns a single vehicle, which he drives a few times a week for personal use on short trips, and a light commercial vehicle that he uses for his business. Under the URUC model we applied, he would pay 23 per cent less because he is a low mileage user outside the city. This is important, because one of the fears regional motorists have, by virtue of the long distances they need to travel, is that they might have to pay more. In fact, the model we applied shows there is a very large cross-subsidy that comes from capital city users and goes across to non–capital city users.

Graham, the second avatar, has two cars, an Audi A4 and a Jeep Cherokee. He drives to work every day along a highly utilised motorway corridor north-west of Sydney and his wife drives short distances in the local area—for example, for the school drop-off. We found for this household a roughly 10 per cent cost increase. For Graham, it is a 45 per cent increase, but there is a substantial decrease for his wife. Again, it shows that, across the household, the outcome is fairer.

Leanne, our third avatar, is a nurse from south-eastern Queensland. Leanne does not drive in the capital city and there is a large cross-subsidy that is flowing through from her road use, resulting in a 23 per cent reduction in her costs. Additionally, she does not travel during peak times.

Table 7.6 shows a comparison of the new charges estimated under the URUC model with charges under the current system. The structure put forward would see no greater cost burden on users as a whole; rather, it would redistribute charges to better reflect true costs (including externalities) and benefits. Before implementation of a similar scheme (or any reform to road user charging), detailed analysis of the price elasticity of demand will be required. However, if structured correctly and priced efficiently, a rational road user charging model would see appropriate and intended shifts in the demand profile.

Table 7.6 Estimate of new road use charges in 2012 dollars

USER	BASE CASE	UNIVERSAL ROAD USER CHARGING			TOTAL NEW CHARGES	% CHANGE
		BASE CHARGE	DISTANCE ROAD USE CHARGE	TIME ROAD USE CHARGE		
Peter						
Vehicle One	$10.97	$0.96	$2.40	$0.00	$3.36	-69.4%
Vehicle Two	$38.07	$0.96	$33.53	$0.00	$34.49	-9.4%
Total	$49.04	$1.92	$35.93	$0.00	$37.85	-22.8%
Graham						
Vehicle One	$26.09	$0.96	$18.04	$18.94	$37.95	45.4%
Vehicle Two	$20.16	$0.96	$5.90	$6.07	$12.93	-35.9%
Total	$46.25	$1.92	$23.94	$25.01	$50.87	10.0%
Leanne						
Vehicle One	$15.61	$0.96	$10.43	$0.57	$11.96	-23.4%
Vehicle Two	$0.00	$0.00	$0.00	$0.00	$0.00	
Total	$15.61	$0.96	$10.43	$0.57	$11.96	-23.4%

Source: Infrastructure Partnerships Australia (2014).

Conclusion

It is easy to be grim about the lack of breadth and ambition in Australia's contemporary policy debate, when even relatively simple reforms with clear national benefits are unable to progress.

But there are positive portents the road transport debate will end up heading in good directions, with the transport policy debate already fundamentally changing in the past few years. The motoring clubs are a key reason for this.

The typical role of user groups in a reform debate is to clamour for more investment, greater subsidies and other unreasonable 'solutions'.

When we released our 2014 report, the CEO of the AAA said the association is in favour of road pricing.

The South Australian Labor Premier, Jay Weatherill (2015), said:

> I propose that we establish a national heavy vehicle road-user charging system run by the Commonwealth … South Australia would be willing to trial different elements of heavy vehicle, road user charging.

The then federal assistant minister for infrastructure and regional development, Jamie Briggs (2015), said: '[U]ltimately, road pricing [is] a fairer way for people to … pay for … roads, to make sure that they continue to be maintained.'

Business has also begun to respond, with Transurban funding a world-leading technology study, assessing how best to capture usage data and give users choice.

These developments show there is a gathering consensus around this issue, and our principal recommendation is that the federal government should direct the Productivity Commission to establish a detailed public inquiry into the funding, regulation and pricing of Australia's road transport market. This inquiry is necessary to give people a say, but also to explain the trade-offs and the overall benefits of road user pricing.

This is not a niche area of government policy or an abstract application of economic theory; rather, it is a fundamental challenge that is entrenched in the price of the goods and services we consume and produce.

This is a goods and services tax (GST)–level change, affecting every household in the country, but the opportunity for these kinds of discussions to be subverted by cheap fear campaigns and other things has effectively been neutered by the involvement of the major logistics groups and the major motoring organisations. We are simply seeking to begin a genuine, honest and collaborative policy reform process for road user charging and funding.

Road pricing and road market reform make an exciting discussion for those who work for government central agencies and the transport agencies within government, and they each have a role to play in promoting intelligent debate. It is a discussion that needs to begin and we need to find acceptable solutions.

We need to give governments the complete picture and also give opposition parties the sense that this is a non-partisan issue. This is a policy issue that needs to be 'kicked off' by calm discussion.

It is a very exciting period in road transport reform because we are fresh out of easy answers—and because of the active involvement and support of the motoring clubs.

But the next step is for the federal government to confirm that the issue of road user charging will advance to a full public inquiry.

A detailed public inquiry is needed to 'pull the teeth' on road pricing. It would let the community begin to have a look underneath the bonnet and see what is wrong; and would mean that, in five or 10 years' time, when the road networks are congested and undermaintained to a point where the heat from the community is such that change can happen, we will have a well-debated, well-understood, well-articulated and well-designed system that is able to move forward to implementation.

If a federal inquiry on road pricing happens, I am bullish that road user charging reform will happen in my lifetime.

References

Briggs, J. (2015). Transcript of speech: Keynote address and luncheon with the Australian British Chamber of Commerce. 9 July. Brisbane. Available from: minister.infrastructure.gov.au/jb/speeches/2015/jbs014_2015.aspx

Department of Infrastructure and Regional Development (DIRD). (2014). *Australian Government Response: Productivity Commission Inquiry Report into Public Infrastructure*. Canberra: Commonwealth of Australia. Available from: infrastructure.gov.au/infrastructure/publications/files/Productivity_Commission_Inquiry_Report_into_Public_Infrastructure.pdf

Industry Commission. (1991). *Rail Transport. Volume I: Report*. Report No. 13, 21 August. Canberra: Australian Government Publishing Service.

Infrastructure Partnerships Australia. (2010). *Role for Road Pricing in the Australian Context*. Discussion paper. Sydney: Infrastructure Partnerships Australia.

Infrastructure Partnerships Australia. (2014). *Road Pricing and Transport Infrastructure Funding: Reform Pathways for Australia*. Discussion paper. Sydney: Infrastructure Partnerships Australia. Available from: www2.deloitte. com/content/dam/Deloitte/au/Documents/public-sector/deloitte-au-ps-road-pricing-transport-infrastructure-funding-260914.pdf

New South Wales Parliament Legislative Council. (2017). Road tolling in New South Wales. Sydney: Portfolio Committee No. 2 – Health and Community Services. Available from: www.parliament.nsw.gov.au/committees/DBAssets/ InquiryReport/ReportAcrobat/6119/Road%20Tolling%20in%20New%20 South%20Wales%20-%20Final%20Report.pdf

Weatherill, J. (2015). South Australia: Essential to the nation's defence. 8 July. National Press Club, Canberra. Available from: www.npc.org.au/speakers/ speaker-2/

8

Lessons from Auckland in road transport planning: Making trade-offs transparent

Peter Winder

During the period 2011–15, Auckland City undertook a concerted effort to find acceptable solutions to the problem that existing funding sources fall well short of the levels of investment necessary to provide the transport outcomes demanded by Aucklanders. This chapter provides an overview of the combined policy and political strategy that was used and reflects on the related lessons it provides. A key focus is the necessity and value of making policy (and political) trade-offs explicit and transparent, and taking the time to ensure that all stakeholders clearly understand both the trade-offs and the associated constraints.

Context

Context is, arguably, everything. A transport planner I worked with once told me that the peak load passenger capacity for a bus in northern China during the winter is one-third less than during the summer, because everyone wears such bulky clothes to survive the cold. It is always important to know and understand the context within which you are working. In this chapter, I will discuss the issue of hypothecation in the context of funding and reinvesting in New Zealand's transport infrastructure.

Since 2008–09, all national transport funding in New Zealand has been hypothecated. For land transport, for example, all vehicle licensing, excise tax and distance-based road user charges for diesel-powered vehicles go straight into the National Land Transport Fund. This is administered by the New Zealand Transport Agency (NZTA), a Crown entity at arm's length from political interference (in theory) that allocates that funding to land transport across the country.

As well as controlling funding, the NZTA also owns the state highway network. This is a clear point of difference with Australia, where major roads are state-owned but often federally prioritised and funded. Local authorities own the remainder of the road network in New Zealand (streets and minor roads), and raise most of their revenue from property taxes, comprising levies on property based on either land value or capital value. In broad terms, local authorities receive matched funding from the NZTA for their approved road and public transport program. There are considerable constraints on and parameters around what projects can be funded and how they must be procured. So it is a slightly different funding framework, and that is part of the context.

The discussion here is focused on Auckland, and again context is important. As a geographer, I tend to think spatially in terms of topography and the physical layout of streets, businesses, homes and offices. Auckland is set on an isthmus between two harbours: Waitemata Harbour to the north-east and Manukau Harbour to the south-west (see Figure 8.1). Otahuhu, the narrowest point between what is in essence the west coast (and the Manukau Harbour) and the east coast of the city, is only 1,200 metres wide—the narrowest point in the country. State Highway 1 forms the principal road corridor connecting the various parts of Auckland. As a matter of historical accident, the railway line also runs more or less along the same route.

Auckland is characterised by low-density settlement, with 1.5 million people spread around the two harbours. As New Zealand's largest city, Auckland is growing quite rapidly, attracting 75 per cent of New Zealand's growth, with two-thirds of that coming from natural population increase. Demographically, Auckland is quite different from the rest of New Zealand, with a large, young and growing population. The population level in most of the rest of the country is static or in decline. This presents particular challenges for the government of the day in terms of how to raise and allocate revenue.

Figure 8.1 Map of Auckland showing major road networks

Source: Based on and including data from Land Information New Zealand, reused under the Creative Commons Attribution 4.0 International licence.

While a system of national hypothecation for the funding of roads has obvious benefits in terms of transparency and equity, trying to raise the national fuel tax to fund expensive road projects in Auckland is a difficult and unpopular political proposition.

Since 2010, a single local authority has administered Auckland, and that has changed things quite dramatically. Having one powerful authority representing the city, rather than the previous eight local authorities, has also changed the context nationally. The unending fighting between local authorities has been removed, as has the opportunity for the central government to play one authority off against another. Amalgamation dramatically changed the balance of power between the central government and the mega local authority, the Auckland Council.

Transport funding gap

Over the next 30 or so years, an important issue for Auckland's growth is the marked gap between the level of future spending required to satisfy the city's expected transport projects (the dotted line in Figure 8.2) and the anticipated actual funding Auckland is likely to receive (the blue line). The red lines shown in Figure 8.2, adapted from a 2014 study (Alternative Transport Funding Project Team 2014), reflect the NZTA's expected program for the next 30 years for Auckland, including the Auckland Council's own program. The blue line aggregates the expected amount to be raised from local property rates by the Auckland Council on current policy settings, plus the proportion of national funding that would arrive in Auckland over that period. The shortfall is significant. To amplify the issue, this funding gap exists in a context where almost every citizen of Auckland thinks not enough is being done to improve transport infrastructure and transport mobility.

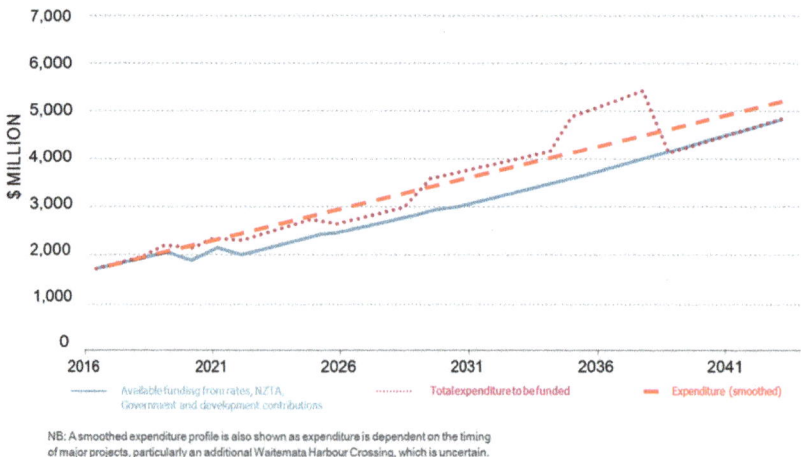

Figure 8.2 Funding gap: $300 million per annum over 30 years

Source: Adapted from Alternative Transport Funding Project Team (2014).

Finding an Auckland solution

With little progress made in previous efforts to address this funding gap, something different was needed. Rather than approaching the question of what is the most appropriate way to raise funds from an academic or esoteric framework, the debate in Auckland has focused on finding politically feasible ways to raise enough money to build the network that is necessary. In the face of a city that is growing rapidly, all of the transport solutions—whether public transport or roads—are expensive. The integrated policy and political process was designed so that it built community support for, and understanding of, the solution as it was developed.

It was obvious the primary challenge was not technical or analytical, but political. Obviously, there are many ways to raise money, all of which are technically feasible. The challenge for jurisdictions is how to get the politics right to make them possible. In Auckland, some work had already been undertaken, with these issues addressed in 2003 by a joint officials group and the associated funding issues fed into the 2007 Auckland Transport Alignment Project. Most of that work, however, has focused on making the right transport investments; trying to get the national government of the day engaged in how to pay for it has been an altogether different challenge.

About three years ago, the Mayor of Auckland asked: How do we change the government's thinking? How do we come up with options that are politically palatable and that will build enthusiasm for the necessary action? The approach adopted—through the combined thinking of the mayor's political strategists, planners and consultants—was to follow a consensus collaborative decision-making model. My role in that process was as the project manager and facilitator.

From the outset it was clear that, if the key issue was to change the politics, what we needed to do was get all the 'movers and shakers' in one room and sort out the politics. So we brought together representatives from all of the major stakeholders. Among the interest groups were some very important players, including unions, employers, infrastructure advocates, the Automobile Association, property investors and the international airport, not to mention local environmentalists, walking and cycling advocates, the tourism industry association and so on. We assembled a 'who's who' of key players in this area and formed a really interesting, challenging, but effective deliberative group. One of the more interesting dynamics to emerge was observing a representative of the child poverty action group advocating staunchly for the least well-off in the community and how that interplayed with both the union movement and local employers and manufacturers, all against a backdrop of working out how to pay more for roads and transport.

Framed in this way, decision-making really became quite simple, albeit not all that quick. We put a group of people in a room and provided a facilitator and whatever resources were necessary to inform them in terms of expert advice and further investigative work, and then asked them to address the issue of road funding on which they would have to reach a consensus. The question they were asked was not how to optimally price the transport network, but how to best raise the extra $300 million a year to build the Auckland Plan's transport network. They were never asked about what, in their opinion, was the best network—and that was really important, because, within the stakeholder group, there were some markedly different views on some of the particular projects that were included in the proposed investments. We would never have achieved consensus on prioritising the projects. What we were able to do instead was work through a platform for raising enough money to implement the whole program.

The first stage to build a consensus involved working through a large number of completely 'blue-sky' or 'off-the-wall' ways to raise money. Topics discussed included regional lotteries, a regional goods and services tax or regional payroll tax, and a raft of things that went in and very quickly went out the other side. A proposal to adopt a betterment tax on improved land values was another of the ideas that went in and disappeared in the first round. We relied on a number of technical reports as to whether these ideas had merit and to work out which of the different options could be dismissed as impractical. During this stage of the process, there was significant engagement with the public on a draft report that enumerated all of the options that had been considered and provided the reasons some had been discarded. At the same time, all of the key stakeholders who were part of the consensus-building group had an obligation to engage with their own member and/or community constituents. This consultation process was part of a very overt campaign to get people focused on the options and choices. The depth of that engagement, for instance, started a number of fascinating debates, such as one that occurred in the union movement about how to charge for transport. It triggered an entrenched political-philosophical debate about the appropriateness or otherwise of user charging of transport, and that debate has continued.

We concluded the first stage of our deliberations with a narrowed field of options, all of which were, in essence, various forms of user charges and conventional mechanisms of rates and fuel taxes (see Table 8.1). We then embarked on a second stage of work, which was designed to take those preferred options and turn them into two funding pathways that could be formally considered by the council and the people of Auckland. Why did we select two funding pathways? As part of the first stage of work, we looked in detail at what other countries had done when they were considering introducing charging schemes, and there were a number of things that stood out. The most blindingly obvious was that when governments go to their communities and ask them whether they would like to pay a new and additional tax, the answer is invariably a definitive 'no'. For obvious reasons, we avoided that trap.

Another thing that was readily apparent to us was that, in the realm of taxation reform, striving for total perfection could be the enemy of the good. Jurisdictions that opted to implement an idealised 'big bang' change or a complicated 'bells and whistles' scheme invariably failed. Hence, we came to the conclusion that it would be far easier to adopt a series of incremental steps in a preferred direction that might take some years to progress. If we were able to get to the first step of introducing a standardised user charge, we reasoned that we would then be able to progressively refine or expand that as a second or third step in the process. It was our view that, over time, we might be able to get closer to an optimum pricing model that charged travellers fairly for usage. If we went out with a complicated scheme straight up, however, set at prices that were optimal, it would almost certainly have failed. All the participants in the consensus-building process, from the very beginning, were conscious that any solution would be not simply a technical question, but rather a political question. How can we get the politics to line up?

Table 8.1 Rates and fuel tax option

	Average annual rates increases	Average annual fuel tax increases (GST incl.)
Annual increases already signalled	2.5% to 3.5% p.a. (Mayoral proposal)	1.6 cents per litre per annum (Draft Government Policy Statement)
	+	+
Annual increase proposed by the IAB for Pathway 1 (dedicated to transport)	0.9% p.a.	1.2 cents per litre per annum
	=	=
Total combined annual increases	3.4% to 4.4% p.a.	2.8 cents per litre p.a.

Source: Alternative Transport Funding Project Team (2014).

The two options that were settled on gave Aucklanders real choices (see Figure 8.3), the first of which was between two different levels of investment: a basic transport network, which was effectively what Auckland could afford based on existing funding sources, or the transport program contained in the Auckland Plan, which required sourcing an additional $300 million a year to implement. So, the first question was very simple: would people prefer the basic option, which would not work, or the expanded option, which would be much more effective? The answer to that question was equally straightforward. Everyone wanted the second option; they were prepared to pay more.

Having established this preference, we then introduced a series of payment options. We asked, if people wanted the more extensive transport plan, how were they prepared to pay for it? The choice we provided Aucklanders was between a flat $2 toll charge for using the motorway system or a combination of increases in property rates and fuel taxes. Reaching a consensus on this question was more of a challenge. The toll charge hit motorists who crossed the isthmus using the designated motorways. The option to increase rates and fuel tax added another 1 per cent per annum (compounding) to people's rates. Combined with the rate increases already contained in the council's budgets, this would result in increases of about 4–4.5 per cent per annum. The proposed fuel tax increase was structured to permanently add about 1.2 cents per litre of petrol.

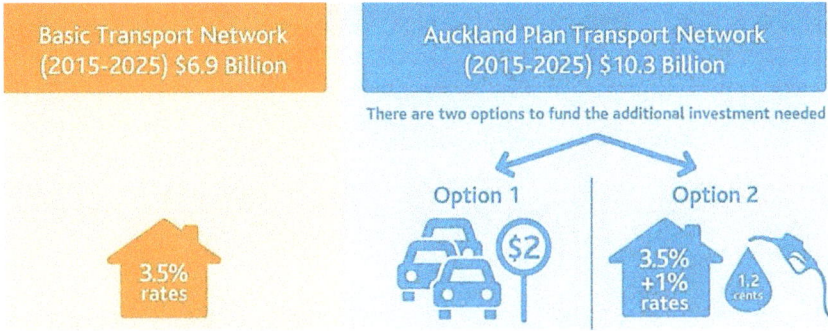

Figure 8.3 Two transport options

Source: Alternative Transport Funding Project Team (2014).

By design, the resulting debate focused entirely on what needed to be raised in Auckland to pay for the city's transport needs. We quite deliberately sidestepped the question of what ought to be done nationally to avoid a debilitating debate about the South Island not wanting to pay for Auckland's infrastructure—an argument Auckland would have lost. We recognised that rates and fuel tax changes were easy to implement, spreading the funding more broadly and delivering critical revenue. Conversely, motorway user charging would be complex, costly to implement and required legislation, but had a range of other economic benefits in terms of aligning cost with benefit.

To impose a local motorway charge, there were two possible user charge options (see Table 8.2). Some of the group wanted to go for simplicity, while others were determined to look at a variable pricing regime. The group eventually managed to agree on a flat rate fee structure. How did we end up there? The answer lies in the fact that the motorway network dominates the transport system in Auckland. A simple charge on the motorway would collect the revenue needed at a reasonably low per use charge. There are quite defined entry and exit points, so tolling is quite straightforward. It is, in essence, a closed system, and it dominates the performance of the network, so it is the easiest solution with the most direct demand consequences. The low level of the necessary charge also helped alleviate the social impact concerns that a number of the group had.

Table 8.2 Motorway user charge option: Two possible approaches to charging

FLAT RATE per use charge				OR	PEAK DEMAND RATE per use charge									
Weekdays		Weekends			Weekdays								Weekends	
					Off peak	AM peak	Off peak	Inter-peak	Off peak	PM peak	Off peak	Nights	6am – 7pm	7pm – 6am
6am – 7pm	7pm – 6am	6am – 7pm	7pm – 6am		6-7 am	7–9 am	9-10 am	10 am – 3pm	3-4 pm	4-6 pm	6-8 pm	8pm – 6am	– 7pm	
$2.00	Free	$2.00	Free		$2.00	$2.80	$2.00	$1.30	$2.00	$2.80	$2.00	Free	$1.30	Free

Source: Alternative Transport Funding Project Team (2014).

In comparing the options, a number of issues were raised, such as transport impacts and the demand for public transport. Figure 8.4 compares the basic network with the impact of the three different charging regimes. Importantly, all of the charging schemes were designed to deliver the same amount of revenue and each delivered the Auckland Plan's transport network. The biggest differences were the future outcomes from the Auckland Plan transport network (compared with the basic network), and obviously this required the additional investment. It is worth noting that, despite the level of investment in the Auckland Plan transport network, our modelling suggested average speeds would get worse over time (see Figure 8.5), so we certainly were not proposing an optimised level of investment. But performance was significantly improved under a motorway user charge compared with rates and fuel tax increases.

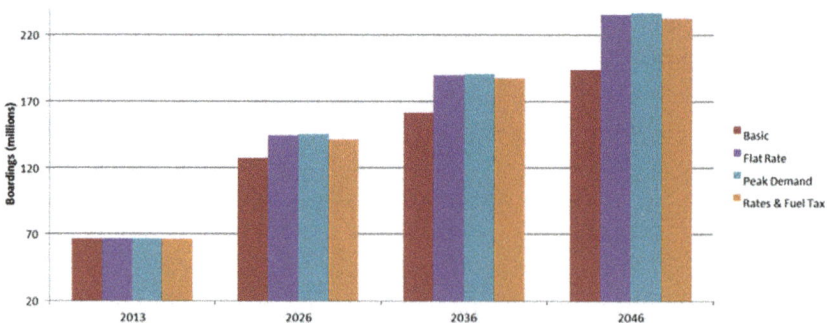

Figure 8.4 Annual passenger transport boardings
Source: Alternative Transport Funding Project Team (2014).

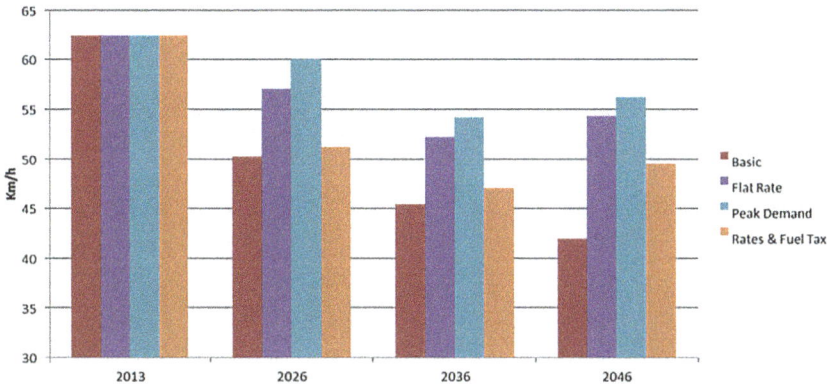

Figure 8.5 Average AM peak speed on the strategic freight network
Source: Alternative Transport Funding Project Team (2014).

Figures 8.6 and 8.7 set out the expected level of congestion under each of the different payment options (with the basic program included as a comparator). Figure 8.6 shows projections of the time spent in morning peak hour congestion and performance under each of the charging options. The outcomes for commuters are significantly better by 2046 with the Auckland Plan transport network, and better again once a variable motorway user charge is introduced to reduce peak demand. Figure 8.7 indicates the similar effects in the inter-peak periods during the day.

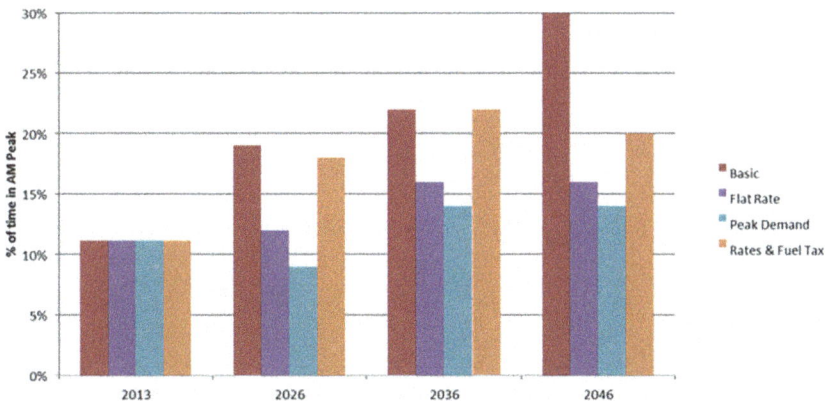

Figure 8.6 Percentage of AM peak spent in severe congestion on the strategic freight network
Source: Alternative Transport Funding Project Team (2014).

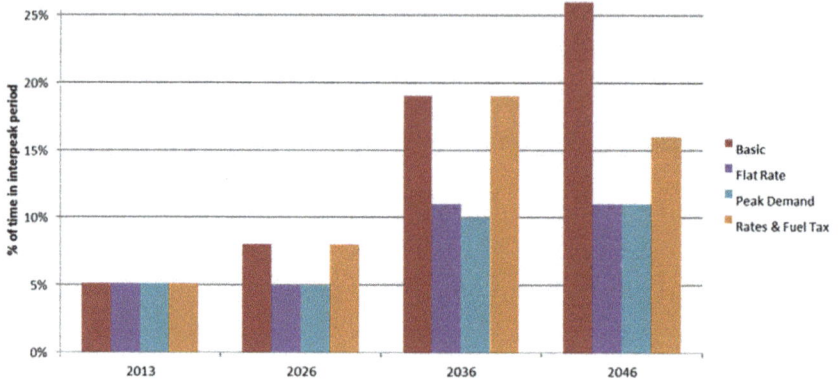

Figure 8.7 Percentage of inter-peak spent in severe congestion on the strategic freight network

Source: Alternative Transport Funding Project Team (2014).

Before making any final decisions, we undertook impact assessments, looking at who wins and who loses. We asked not only which charging option we should adopt, but also who was most likely to pay. We were able to determine that businesses would pay 34 per cent of the rates and fuel tax increases and, if a motorway toll was introduced, they would pay 41–46 per cent of the charge (see Table 8.3). The analysis indicated, however, that the benefits to business exceeded the costs. It was an indication of the strength of the consensus-building process that all the business representatives in the consultative group were able to say: 'Yes, we can "swallow" that.'

The average impact on households is much the same between the two schemes, but the incidence of the charges is quite different. Drivers who are regular users pay a significantly greater proportion of the motorway user charge. Moreover, vulnerable households end up paying more under either pathway. In terms of economic impacts, we had interesting and ongoing debates about how these would be calculated, and determining the base case. But the bottom line was that a better return was delivered by implementing the motorway user charge than with rates and fuel tax increases.

Table 8.3 Fairness/impact of charging options

Rates and Fuel Tax	Motorway User Charge
• Business pays 34% • Savings to business exceed costs • Avg cost per h'hold $348 pa by 2026 • Extra rates apply irrespective of use • Vulnerable h'holds pay 15% of charges • For 12% of vulnerable h'holds increased charges are more than 1.75% of net income • Changing travel behaviour will not reduce costs • Tolls on only some new roads is unfair	• Business pays 41%-46% • Savings to business exceed costs • Avg cost per h'hold $345 pa by 2026 • Regular M'way users (8% of h'holds) pay 26% of charges – $1500 pa per h'hold • Other h'holds pay as little as $150 pa • Vulnerable h'holds pay 11% of charges • For 7% of vulnerable h'holds increased charges are more than 1.75% of net income • Changing travel behaviour can reduce costs

Source: Alternative Transport Funding Project Team (2014).

The consensus-building group reported its findings to the Auckland Council, which then put the two choices to the people of Auckland as part of their three-yearly long-term planning process. In a month, through a large consultation process, the council received 15,000 submissions on this issue, and, of those, as shown in Figures 8.8 and 8.9, more than 50 per cent supported the Auckland Plan transport network as opposed to the basic network. Unfortunately, during the consultation process, Generation Zero, a young people's lobby group, started advocating for another network altogether, which had the effect of diluting somewhat the clarity of the message delivered by the consultation.

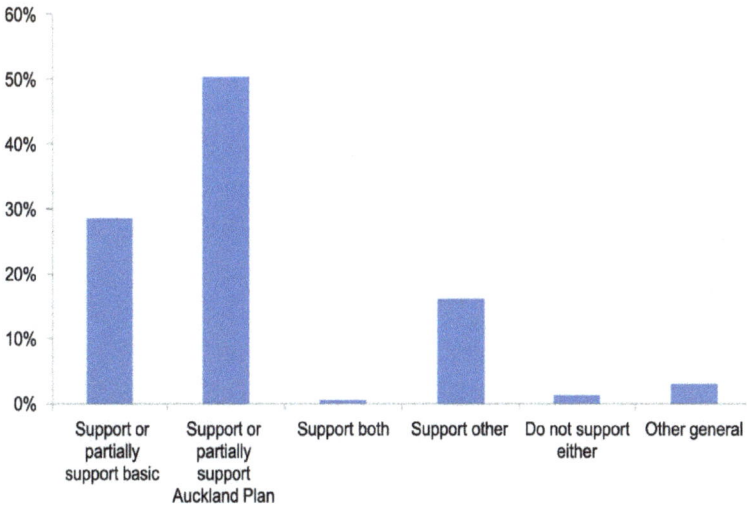

Figure 8.8 Submissions relating to the proposed networks
Source: Alternative Transport Funding Project Team (2014).

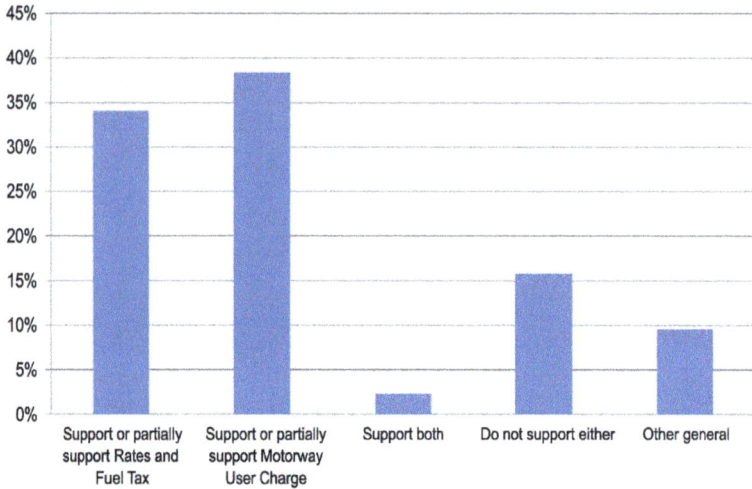

Figure 8.9 Submissions relating to proposed funding options
Source: Alternative Transport Funding Project Team (2014).

Figure 8.8 shows there was more popular support for the motorway user charge than for an increase in rates and fuel tax. Unfortunately, a material number of people bought into the 'other' network and therefore concluded that an increase in cost was not necessary. In parallel, the council conducted a random survey of 5,000 Aucklanders that showed similar results (Tables 8.4 and 8.5), but with a stronger preference for the Auckland Plan because in this survey the third alternative was not in the choice set for respondents. In terms of a preference for charging frameworks, there was evidence of significant support for the motorway user charge.

Table 8.4 Preferred transport network survey results

Preferred transport network	Support
Basic transport network	32%
Auckland Plan transport network	58%
Neither	5%
Don't know / other	5%

Source: Alternative Transport Funding Project Team (2014).

Table 8.5 Preferred funding option survey results

Preferred funding option	Support
Motorway User Charge	57%
Fuel taxes and rates	31%
Neither	10%
Don't know	2%

Source: Alternative Transport Funding Project Team (2014).

So what did we learn from all of this? The surveys showed that by deliberately making this a public discussion about choices, and in turn making both the choices and their consequences explicit, we were able to get to a rather different point than critics of the process had expected. We arrived at a point where we had the consensus-building group— and all of the key stakeholders—more or less saying this is the right way to go. We had the public of Auckland saying yes, we are prepared to accept something different to improve transport outcomes.

At this point, it was the political reaction that was all important. The Auckland Council does not have the legislative ability to introduce road user charges or a motorway charging scheme for highways in its own jurisdiction and the central government indicated it was not yet convinced by Auckland's arguments. As a result, the council resolved to continue its advocacy efforts and implement a targeted rate in the interim to bridge some of the gap. There remained majority support on the council to implement a motorway user charge and to continue to argue the funding issue with the national government.

The national government, however, remains unconvinced. Other participants who attended the 'Shifting the Transport Infrastructure Debate in Australia' workshop have mentioned a time frame of three hours between a policy being floated and the government saying 'no'. However, through this deliberative process, there had been a succession of 'nos'. The period of lapsed time between when Auckland Council releases something and when the national government says 'no' is getting longer, and the reasons for the 'no' are changing and diminishing. To maintain progress, the Auckland Council and the national government have agreed on the need to set up another study, the Auckland Transport Alignment Project (ATAP). Importantly, the terms of reference for that work include both parties agreeing with the suite of projects *as well as* agreeing on funding. So the government is continuing to materially shift its position in response to what Auckland Council has done, to the point that now it is willing to formally consider funding, whereas previously it would not.

ATAP remains a work in progress. Following the local and general elections in 2016 and 2017 (respectively), the original ATAP has been updated to take into account the latest population forecasts (Ministry of Transport 2018). Whether the government will be prepared to move on something as significant as this in the year-long window between the two elections remains a big question.

In conclusion, my principal message from the Auckland case study is that it is possible to discuss and scope many items of important public policy considered controversial, unpopular and even esoteric. If, however, those involved cannot take people with them and therefore change the politics associated with their proposals and win support, nothing much will happen. At the end of the day, it's all about the politics.

References

Alternative Transport Funding Project Team. (2014). *Funding Auckland's Transport Future: Two Pathways*. Auckland: Auckland Council. Available from: www.shapeauckland.co.nz/media/1182/section-113-alternative-transport-funding-informationa4.pdf (accessed 23 May 2015).

Ministry of Transport. (2018). *Auckland Transport Alignment Project*. Wellington: Ministry of Transport. Available from: www.transport.govt.nz/land/auckland/atap

Section 4: Turning theory into practice

9

Winning public support for transport reforms

Gary Banks

> It ought to be remembered that there is nothing more difficult to take in hand, more perilous to conduct, or more uncertain in its success, than to take the lead in the introduction of a new order of things. For the innovator has for enemies all those who have done well under the old conditions, and only lukewarm defenders in those who may do well under the new.
>
> — Niccolo Machiavelli, 1513

The reformer's dilemma has rarely been more eloquently or succinctly put than in Machiavelli's much-cited observation in *The Prince*. Written half a millennium ago, it shows this problem is neither new nor confined to democracies. That said, more recent experience suggests a corollary to Machiavelli's axiom, which could be expressed in similar terms: there is often nothing easier for a government than to make *bad* policies, for it can count on strong support from those who profit and little opposition from those who lose.

Many of the policies needing reform today were introduced in precisely such circumstances. Once in place, of course, such policies can become politically very hard to withdraw—and that is the nub of the problem we face today in securing key transport policy reforms.

Expanding a little, the reality is that, almost by definition, structural reform generally entails losses for some groups. These are typically much more concentrated within the community and individually significant to its members than are the consequent gains from reform, notwithstanding their much larger overall magnitude. It follows that those with most at stake, and therefore having the loudest political voice, will normally be the losers, not the winners from reform. And to those not following things too closely, they have persuasive arguments, including the ability to identify actual workers in specific electorates at risk of losing their jobs and livelihood (the 'phone book' test).

The asymmetries confounding reform do not stop there. Significant ones exist within government itself—notably, the division along sectoral lines of bureaucratic structures. While having departments 'responsible' for such sectors as manufacturing, agriculture and mining, or for certain groups in society or for the environment facilitates policy knowledge and program expertise in such areas, it can lead to fragmented information systems and an inability to see the 'big picture'. Central agencies have a broader remit, but often lack the detailed knowledge to act as an effective policy counterweight.

The automobile industry has traditionally been one of the most successful beneficiaries of this asymmetric political economy favouring government preferment (second perhaps only to the Pharmacy Guild), with workers, bosses and sponsoring departments united in common cause.

If anything, the present political contours are making the conditions for successful reform even tougher than they were. Meaningful reform initiatives (ones that actually live up to the name) are getting harder to contemplate and, especially, consummate. There are a number of interacting forces at work.

A key one relates to what I have been calling 'Washminster'. Changes within our political-bureaucratic structures have seen the balance of power in policy development shifting decidedly from the department (with its technical expertise) to the minister's office. This drift has ironically coincided with a loss of policy capability in ministerial offices as careerist political staffers, often with political aspirations of their own, replace policy experts close to the minister. The consequent ascendancy of politics over policy has been exacerbated by the advent of 'new media', with its insatiable daily need for content that 'sells'. Sensationalism, conflict and faux controversy are its currency. This fans the 'oppositionism' that has emerged with a vengeance in our parliaments—for who could reasonably expect to get media attention for agreeing with the government?

There is currently a presumption that politicians should respond immediately to issues, making decisions in time for the daily news cycle. Ministers themselves feel they have to react quickly, if only to preempt a potential opposition attack that might get first run in the media.

The problems are compounded as the modern media machine interacts with increasingly fickle and volatile electorates. Old political loyalties and habit voting have largely broken down. It was once accepted that no more than 10–20 per cent of voters would be 'swingers', with most of the electorate having a fairly enduring sense of party identification (and a significant number being 'rusted on'). Recent surveys and studies suggest that swinging or floating voters may now constitute up to 40 per cent of the electorate. In other words, proportionately more votes are 'up for grabs' than ever before. At the same time, growing affluence and abundant information mean the electorate has more things of concern to them politically. And vested interests have ready access to electronic soapboxes that provide wide reach but little real scrutiny.

Lessons from past structural reform successes

While the environment just described is undoubtedly a tougher one for reformers than in the past, the obstacles to structural reform have never been trivial. Admittedly, some of the key reforms, such as reducing industry protection, were not *technically* difficult—and in that sense involved 'low-hanging fruit'—but all faced considerable political hurdles. Indeed, opposition to tariff reform was fierce. The approaches used to secure structural reforms in the past therefore, in my view, remain relevant to our current challenges.

The standout structural reform was the National Competition Policy (NCP), which yielded important gains to the Australian community. In its policy coverage and cross-jurisdictional reach, its achievements were without precedent internationally and it continues to be lauded in forums such as the Organisation for Economic Co-operation and Development (OECD). The NCP was confronted by all the adverse political and administrative asymmetries noted previously, as well as the additional complexity of securing agreement among several governments. In enabling the market to occupy areas where competition had previously been excluded, the NCP was essentially seeking to withdraw longstanding 'entitlements'. So how was this achieved?

A Productivity Commission review of the NCP in 2005 came up with three overarching success factors:

- Recognition by governments and oppositions across the country that there was a problem and that changes were needed if Australians were to sustain high standards of living.

- Broad acceptance of the solutions, some of which were quite innovative. The notion of reversing the onus of proof in relation to the competition test—requiring the recipient of a regulatory barrier to make a national interest case for retaining it—was revolutionary in its overturning of historical convention.

- Implementation arrangements gave careful consideration to the structuring of incentives and governance arrangements for implementation, with the National Competition Council central to this architecture.

Each of these could be seen simply as conditions that need to be satisfied for any successful reform. The more fundamental question is how they were satisfied. The commission's report again found three key contributors.

First was the existence of credible evidence and analysis about both the extent of the policy problem and the likely benefits from mooted reforms. While the Hilmer review (1993) was instrumental in this, it had the benefit of earlier inquiries and research by the Industry Commission, the Economic Planning Advisory Commission (EPAC), the Australian Bureau of Agricultural and Resource Economics (ABARE) and other well-respected independent bodies. These often involved not only research, but also the testing of findings and policy ideas in public forums.

Second, there was strong technical and advisory support within key departments and political offices. I have stated previously that the calibre of senior public servants and ministerial advisors has never been higher than it was in those years. This meant that policy champions had the ear of ministers, in advancing the ideas coming out of inquiries or reviews and refined through the bureaucracy. This was reinforced by new coordination processes across ministries and jurisdictions.

Third, and most important, was the quality of political leadership, at both federal and state levels, including the ability to explain and promote the idea of structural reform and the community-wide benefits that would flow from it, notwithstanding the adjustment problems for some. It enabled a compelling narrative to be consistently advocated over a long period. It is not enough to have the right answer (as the opposition Liberal Party's 'Fightback' platform showed). Good policy has to be explained effectively to the public to make a difference. This is, above all, the task of the political leadership.

These elements were all mutually reinforcing. Good process, careful program design, effective leadership and a strong, consistent narrative were the hallmarks of the NCP's success. Expressed in this way, the fact successful outcomes resulted is not surprising. Indeed, the OECD has identified similar factors in the reform successes of a range of countries.

Winston Churchill is said to have remarked that a government should never 'waste a good crisis' as an opportunity to advance hard policy decisions. Australia's reforms had more to do with a well-engineered sense of crisis than the real thing. Former treasurer Paul Keating's famous evocation of a 'banana republic' in a radio interview was one instance (echoing Lee Kwan Yew's equally impactful 'white trash' warning of a few years earlier (Clare 2015)). Similarly, treasurer Peter Costello (2004) was able to convince the public that a looming crisis awaited if we failed to prepare for the 'destiny' of an ageing population. In neither case were existing economic settings in a desperate state, but the ability to project what lay ahead and to provoke public discussion about this and the actions required to avert the problems constituted a compelling reform narrative. (There are other examples I could cite, including Costello's '$8 billion black hole' (Davidson 2005).)

Another feature of successful reform leadership was the ability to anticipate and genuinely address potential adjustment costs. If this factor is ignored, it has the potential to derail reform initiatives. Australians have a deeply ingrained sense of fairness, reflected in welfare entitlements that exceed those in most countries. Reforms bringing community-wide benefits still need to pay attention to the losers, especially redundant workers. The incentive payments to the states and territories were partly predicated on providing the fiscal wherewithal for this. In addition—and apart from the general safety nets—programs for retraining or relocation were devised in conjunction with the reforms. (It has to be said though that the reality fell somewhat short of the rhetoric, which, in the end, arguably inhibited the full implementation of the NCP agenda.)

Is transport reform tougher?

These observations about the success factors in the NCP provide a long, but hopefully relevant, introduction to the question of 'winning support for transport reform'. The transport policy reform agenda is very similar to that of the NCP itself. It involves questions of governance and asset management, the structures for funding and user charging and the extent to which governments retain equity and control. It is also about reducing regulation that is anticompetitive or otherwise raises costs or inhibits productivity. And, looking to the future, it is about securing a better basis for informing investment decisions, particularly in relation to allocation and timing.

If the transport reform agenda is indeed comparable to national competition policy reform, one might ask why more headway has not been made? After all, there have been several public inquiries and reviews making a cogent case for reform, akin to the Hilmer review, including some by the Productivity Commission, as well as a number of special taskforces. We have also seen considerable high-level government attention being paid to the issues, particularly in relation to funding aspects. And we briefly even had a prime minister proclaiming himself 'the infrastructure prime minister' (Abbott 2013).

Yet, spending aside, we have seen less progress on the structural reform dimensions than in other areas of public infrastructure: less governance reform (with most entities still embedded in departmental structures), less contestability and less cost-reflective pricing. Understanding why that is so is obviously the key to moving forward. It seems unlikely it is because transport is an inherently more complex policy area than, say, energy, water or telecommunications, as anyone familiar with telecommunications would attest for a start. But if not *technically* more complex, could it be said that the *politics* are more challenging?

In considering the political dimensions, it is useful to examine the potential 'blockers' to specific reforms. Unsurprisingly, the 'usual suspects' loom large.

For a start, when it comes to reforming *governance* arrangements (corporatisation, privatisation or even commercialisation), politicians, existing provider organisations, the unions and consumers each have their own concerns about loss of control or loss of income, or both.

In the *regulatory* space, as noted, incumbents can be expected to oppose regulatory changes that will increase competitive pressures. And labour unions often resist moves to enhance organisational 'flexibility' as code for loss of entitlements.

Vested interests typically pursue objectives other than *efficiency* for capital spending. And governments themselves tend to be attracted less to smaller bottleneck investments—even those with a high pay-off—than to higher-profile greenfield projects.

But the strongest opposition has arisen in relation to *user charging* for roads. Traditionally, the public has seen roads as a free good, funded through less transparent fuel excise and other taxation, rather than direct pricing. So proposals to introduce cost-reflective pricing are bound to face broad opposition, particularly from those paying more as a result.

The obstacles to these reforms, while challenging, are not so different to those for other areas of infrastructure that progress should not be possible. Even in the most challenging area of road pricing, users are becoming accustomed to the principle of 'user pays' from moves in other service areas (such as water) and have clearly accepted the logic for toll roads. And, given roads are not really 'free' anyway, making a compelling case for moving to a more efficient way of paying for them, provided arrangements can be shown to be 'fair', should not be so hard. Indeed, considerable headway has already been made, with reports by the Productivity Commission and Infrastructure Partnerships Australia showing the way forward. At least the technological hurdles are now surmountable, such that charging based on where and when a vehicle actually uses the road network can be accurately determined. Provided there can be some assurance that resulting revenue will flow into improved road services (admittedly no simple matter institutionally), support from business at least could be assured.

Advancing the transport reform agenda

The biggest challenges currently have more to do with the general deterioration in the climate for structural reforms, described earlier. While these may call for new tactics and tools, the broad approach that worked so well for us in the past should remain central. The dual preconditions for success remain securing broad agreement on why reform is needed and on the reforms that will deliver the greatest public value.

Too often in recent times governments have sought to truncate this two-step process, pursuing the 'what' before ensuring the 'why' is understood and accepted. Admittedly, building public understanding of the need for change can be difficult. It cannot be achieved overnight. It requires persistence and repetition. (Former prime minister John Howard recently remarked in an interview that 'a treasurer must be in the media every day … Making the case for change, being one of the government's most effective communicators' (Bowen 2014).)

Arm's-length policy reviews can provide crucial support. In particular, credible independent estimates of the costs of the status quo and of the gains from reform constitute handy rhetorical assets for a government. Compared with the earlier Hilmer review process, however, it is not clear that more recent reviews in the transport area have done enough to convince people there is a real problem. Or, perhaps more accurately, it is not clear that governments have taken sufficient advantage of the opportunity they presented to make a compelling case.

Only once the need for change is broadly accepted can specific reform proposals be effectively prosecuted. These need to lay out not only the gains from change, but also the likely incidence of both gains and losses, whether the latter would be mitigated in some way and, if not, why not. The public will focus on the losers (encouraged by the media and the losers themselves) and will ultimately make a judgement about whether the proposed reforms seem fair. This is more likely to the extent that reform processes have allowed people to voice their concerns and whether the government is judged to have listened. (Listening is often more important in the end than whether the government actually agrees.)

Because there is always an element of uncertainty as well as disruption in any significant reform proposal, the public will naturally be risk-averse. Pilot projects and the phasing in of initiatives can help allay concerns, as well as pointing to potential design improvements ahead of a wider rollout. (We heard the instructive example of Sweden, where road pricing was widely opposed at the outset, but, following a carefully staged implementation process, eventually received a 70 per cent approval rating from the public.)

In Australia, there is of course the additional difficulty of securing acceptance and agreement across our federation. Previous examples of reforms that have stalled or failed have often arisen because there has not been agreement about the problem or the proffered solution (or both) in the first place. In some cases, a federal government has sought to proceed without properly consulting the states. The outcome in most such cases, unsurprisingly, has been failure. It should be obvious therefore that much transport reform, particularly road pricing, stands no chance without securing collaboration and cooperation across jurisdictions.

Summing up

To conclude, desirable transport reform is challenging—for reasons I have outlined—and it would be easy to become pessimistic about its prospects. But the specific challenges are not really more daunting than in some other areas of infrastructure reform. And much good work establishing the case for reform has already been done.

The real question is whether political leaders are up to the task, in an environment that has become ever more challenging for far-sighted reform. There is mounting evidence that they are not; however, there are also a few shards of light in the gloom. For example, the fact the most recent NSW election was essentially fought on an important infrastructural reform issue, and that the government managed to prevail notwithstanding orchestrated opposition from 'the usual suspects', provides some grounds for optimism. Then there is the impressive reformist record of the previous New Zealand Government, which, contrary to Jean-Claude Juncker's aphorism, not only knew what to do, but also managed to get re-elected— not once, but twice. The New Zealand experience reinforces the lessons from Australia's own past, that the key to governments winning public support is a credible and well-argued case that reforms will actually make life better for a country's citizens. That does not seem too much to ask.

References

Abbott, T. (2013). Tony Abbott's campaign launch speech: full transcript. 25 August. Brisbane. Available from: www.smh.com.au/politics/federal/tony-abbotts-campaign-launch-speech-full-transcript-20130825-2sjhc.html

Bowen, C. (2014). *The Money Men: Australia's Twelve Most Notable Treasurers.* Melbourne: Melbourne University Press.

Clare, J. (2015). Why Australia is in danger of becoming Asia's digital banana republic. *Business Insider*, 24 October. Available from: www.businessinsider.com.au/why-australia-is-in-danger-of-becoming-asias-digital-banana-republic-2015-10

Costello, P. (2004). Speech: Australia's demographic challenges. 25 February. Marriott Hotel, Sydney. Available from: www.petercostello.com.au/speeches/2004/2066-australia-s-demographic-challenges

Davidson, K. (2005). A charter of budget dishonesty. *The Age*, June 9. Available from: www.theage.com.au/news/Kenneth-Davidson/A-charter-of-budget-dishonesty/2005/06/08/1118123894921.html

Hilmer, F. G., Rayner, M. R. and Taperell, G. Q. (1993). *National Competition Policy: Report by the Independent Committee of Inquiry.* Canberra: Commonwealth of Australia. Available from: ncp.ncc.gov.au/docs/National%20Competition%20Policy%20Review%20report,%20The%20Hilmer%20Report,%20August%201993.pdf

Machiavelli, N. (1988). *The Prince*, ed. Quentin Skinner and Russell Price. Cambridge; New York: Cambridge University Press.

Productivity Commission. (2005). *Review of National Competition Policy Reforms: Productivity Commission Inquiry Report.* Canberra: Productivity Commission. Available from: www.pc.gov.au/inquiries/completed/national-competition-policy/report/ncp.pdf

10

Assessing the likelihood of proposed reform pathways to road pricing in Australia: Do they necessarily involve 'diabolical politics'?

John Wanna

Over recent years, a number of detailed official reports have been publicly released advocating various options for a more sustainable, efficient and transparent road charging regime.[1] These policy reports by highly reputable bodies in the public and private sectors, including input from specialist parliamentary committees, argue, principally, that the present road funding arrangements are inadequate and unsustainable, distortionary, not related to the efficient use of road networks and corridors and do not allow sensible investment decisions to be made over the longer term. They have not necessarily been adopted as definitive policy pronouncements by any jurisdictional level of government in Australia. Mostly, these reports are critical of the existing complexities and messiness in the provision and

---

1   These public reports are in addition to considerable work within the levels of government by departments of infrastructure, transport and treasury. There has also been work directly focused on road user charging commissioned by the Transport and Infrastructure Council of federal, state and territory transport ministers. Some of this research-based material is made public, especially as information papers, discussion papers, reports and statistical updates. These public reports are listed in the reference list for this chapter.

upkeep of roads, which currently involve all three levels of government, with no one taking responsibility for the system-wide aspects of the network, especially investment priorities and the design and management of the road asset base. The reformist reports take the form of 'green paper'-style discussion papers intended to inform the community and setting out selected options for public consultation. This chapter considers a selection of these more influential reports from the recent past and examines the prospects for and feasibility of their ideas and reform proposals.

Limitations of the present system of road pricing and funding

So what, fundamentally, is wrong with the present system of road funding?

- First, the existing array of pricing and cost-recovery mechanisms is indirect, unnecessarily complicated and politically messy, involving multiple but separate jurisdictions.

- Second, funds raised by state and territory governments do not closely relate to actual usage, and excise levies are only approximately related to usage.

- Third, there is no link between these various charges on vehicles and the costs of providing and maintaining our present road network.

- Fourth, road funding by governments is considered to be an essentially political arrangement, inherently arbitrary and inefficient for both road users and network asset management.

- Fifth, the projected funds generated by road and fuel charges are considered insufficient to fund the existing road network going forward and to meet future infrastructure needs.

Presently, road users pay various levies into the consolidated revenue accounts of different jurisdictions—namely, a series of fixed state-based access charges including licence fees and vehicle registration levies, plus a mixture of consumption-based levies on various fuels collected by the Commonwealth Government through its excise taxation powers (although fuel excise is not a fee-for-service charge). State governments also impose stamp duties on new vehicles and fees for new licence plates, while local governments collect parking levies. In addition, the Commonwealth imposes fringe benefits taxes on the private usage of company-provided vehicles, some luxury car taxes and customs duties. In total, Australian governments raise approximately $30 billion in road-related revenues, but spend about $25 billion on road-related funding, much of which is in the form of recurrent funding by state and territory governments, although major road investment is a charge to the capital budget and is often borrowed. Over time, governments tend to increase charges on fuel and levies on vehicles when they want a revenue increase, not necessarily when they want to invest more in roads.

Significantly, these levies as proxies for road user charges are not necessarily tied to the provision of better roads or the more efficient use of road transport networks. Governments can spend more or less on roads than these various levies return to the Treasury. As such, there is no apparent relationship here and the level of funding committed to road investments in government budgets can vary enormously from year to year, especially at the Commonwealth level.

Other factors may also drive investment in roads—not necessarily the condition of the existing road network or demands for new roads. Hence, governments in the different jurisdictions can vary spending aggregates depending on their own pressing priorities and funding obtained from other sources. They can also spend more or less on infrastructure for reasons not related to actual usage patterns. One factor is countercyclical fiscal policy, where governments reduce spending when economic growth is high and increase spending when economic business cycles decline. Employment creation associated with road building or maintenance plays a significant role in this policy framework. Moreover, servicing the needs of population growth (and location) is an underlying but ongoing pressure on demand for new roads; and the impact of that population growth varies by region and between regions over time as they experience growth or decline. Improving economic access through road infrastructure can be an important component of regional development policies determining the specifics of road construction.

Another complicating factor driving road expenditure is that such spending across the public sector remains a highly politically driven process, with little transparency or rationale. Governments decide not only how much to allocate to roads from their resources, but also the location and types of roads to be built or extended. Systemic integration or interoperability may not be foremost in their thinking. Road building, road extensions and road maintenance programs (including road widening, increased lanes, tunnels, bridges, 'blackspots', country town bypasses and so on) are subject to the whims of governments of the day seeking re-election or placating local interests. Commonwealth transfers to the states and territories for roads and repairs (and to local governments for road repair) remain allocated under the tied grants provision in the Constitution (Section 96 on payments) and usually come with conditionality or earmarked priorities attached.

A consequence of this interplay of factors is that irregular patterns of investment in roads tend to prevail. For instance, the Commonwealth committed just $2 billion to road funding in 2001, increased funding in 2005–06 to more than $5 billion—up from $2.47 billion the year before—and dropped back to $2.96 billion in 2006–07. In 2011–12, federal road funding rose to almost $8 billion, before dropping back to less than $5 billion by 2015. Such variability shifts costs and makes planning uncertain.

Beside the disconnect between road user charging and investment in the asset network, many of the publicly available reports, referred to above, address the inadequacies of the revenue-raising instruments themselves. A common criticism is that fixed licence fees and vehicle registration fees are crude instruments for funding roads and make no allowance for the intensity of usage by road users. These fees simply *entitle* usage, but in no way relate to actual usage.

A second criticism is that the substantial reliance on fuel excise from fuels such as petrol, diesel, ethanol, biodiesel and fuel blends is not a feasible long-term tax and is incapable of generating sufficient funds for the road network. Projections suggest that total excise revenues since the 1990s have been declining as a proportion of gross domestic product (GDP) and as a proportion of total receipts to the Commonwealth (Infrastructure Australia 2013).[2] Indeed, one influential report noted that the overall amount of money raised from fuel excise has been decreasing since 2003 and is projected to decrease even further into the future (from $7.5 billion to approximately $5 billion) (Graham and Reedman 2015). Moreover, the shift to fuel-efficient vehicles and alternative fuel types (and even electric-powered vehicles) has further exacerbated this trend.

---

2   Infrastructure Australia found that fuel excise revenues as a percentage of GDP halved from 2001–02 to 2013. Although note must be taken that the goods and services tax (GST) elicited from fuel sales (including the levy being applied to the excise amount—that is, 'double taxation') that otherwise would be an additional 'fuel tax' is not included in the fuel excise figures, nor is it allocated to states for road building/maintenance.

In terms of the revenue sources keeping pace with expenditure requirements, fuel excise was not indexed from 2001 until 2014. Unless the Commonwealth elected to increase the fuel excise charge from 38 cents per litre of fuel to closer to 60 cents (as estimated by Infrastructure Australia), this source of funds is likely to continue to decline and not keep pace with infrastructural spending needs. And such a large hike in the rate of excise would not only feed into inflation and production costs, but also raise significant equity issues for those who have to travel great distances or require transport in their line of work.

If these criticisms of the limitations of the existing arrangements are widely accepted, what are the proposed solutions or remedies to this sorry state?

Evaluating the main proposals from the reform advocates

In recent years, there have been at least six major reports into aspects of road pricing and interconnected issues of road funding and demand moderation. Their principal arguments, conclusions and recommendations are set out below.

The recent review of Australia's future tax system (2008–09), led by then Treasury head Ken Henry, examined two main aspects of funding road usage or reducing demand on usage: 1) measures to reduce urban congestion in major cities; and 2) the introduction of mass–distance–location pricing for heavy vehicles to ensure they pay for their marginal road wear costs. The report predicted congestion costs to the economy would exceed $20 billion by 2020, falling mainly on Sydney, Melbourne and Brisbane road users, and would continue to grow unless 'location specific congestion charges [that] vary according to the time of day' were implemented (Henry et al. 2010: 53). It criticised the existing array of taxes attributable to road users for being too inexplicit and indiscriminate. It argued that Australia should move from 'indiscriminate taxes to efficient prices ... to leverage the value of its existing transport infrastructure' (Henry et al. 2010: 53). It argued for a 'single institution to lead road tax reform, and ensure implementation', nominated by and presumably answerable to the Council of Australian Governments (COAG) (Henry et al. 2010: 93).

Although the report mentioned demand-driven pricing, it did not endorse a system of direct road pricing; rather, it pushed for congestion charges while leaving open the question of whether fuel excise should be used as the principal basis for road funding. The logic of this report, in other words, was that fuel excise and vehicle registration charges should be phased out over time and replaced with 'more efficient road user charges', although the report chose not to spell out what these should be, other than mentioning congestion pricing (Henry et al. 2010: 93, 398). Furthermore, one recommendation suggested that 'revenue from fuel tax imposed for general government purposes should be replaced over time with revenue from more efficient broad-based taxes', which could include consumption taxes or even the GST (Henry et al. 2010: Recommendation 65). Such a move would provide road funding with a more robust community-based growth tax (making funding more sustainable into the future) but would not constitute a direct user charge, and would not in itself constitute a congestion charge.

A Victorian parliamentary committee inquiry (Road Safety Parliamentary Committee 2010) largely accepted the status quo in terms of the current revenue-raising regimes, but argued for more dedicated spending on roads. It did not argue for direct user charging, but instead opted to retain the federal fuel excise levy while arguing for greater hypothecation of road-generated revenues (earmarking funds collected purely for investment in roads). It was reasonably satisfied with the Commonwealth collecting excise on fuel (or thought the prospects of any change away from excise charging were not great), but did not endorse direct user charging. It recommended that 50 per cent of federal fuel excise should be hypothecated and, of this, 60 per cent should be earmarked for local roads, with the other 40 per cent going to state roads. Quixotically, the committee hoped the 'hypothecated portion of fuel excise revenue was both raised and spent by the states without the need for federal government involvement' (Road Safety Parliamentary Committee 2010: 63). The committee, which was charged mainly with investigating road safety issues, urged that the hypothecated funding arrangements be reviewed after five years.

In November 2011, the NSW Parliament announced an inquiry into road access pricing, which commenced in December 2012 and conducted public hearings on one day in May 2013. There was a particular focus on heavy vehicle usage, with rail lobbyists urging the committee to endorse competitive neutrality between transport sectors. The committee produced a report but did not release it before the March 2015 election because of the political sensitivities involved. The chair of the committee, Charles Casuscelli, said the committee had been impressed by a popularly supported pricing scheme introduced by the US state of Oregon, which charged motorists 1.5 cents per mile travelled on roads (Saulwick 2014). Parliamentary committees in most other states and territories have generally eschewed looking into road pricing per se, and instead have tended to focus on arguing for adequate levels of funding, better local road funding, highlighting the parlous state of rural roads and road safety issues. It seems that industry lobbyists and think tanks have been more courageous than parliamentary committees in being prepared to investigate various pricing options (see, for instance, Australasian Railways Association 2010; Terrill and and Emslie 2016; Terrill et al. 2016).

Perhaps the most comprehensive and influential set of reform proposals to have emerged in recent years was the Productivity Commission's major report into *Public Infrastructure* (2014), which included a specific section on the 'reform in the roads sector' that argued Australia needed to 'move to alternative institutional models in the roads sector' and recommended the establishment of a 'corporatized public road agency model'. According to the commission:

> [T]he new model should provide the opportunity and incentives to consider future direct road user charges, which would facilitate more effective asset utilisation and more rigorous assessment of new investments. (Productivity Commission 2014: 303)

The commission urged governments across Australia to adopt a 'clear price signal for road use'.

However, while it admitted that 'ideally, there would be a unified system of user charging for all vehicles that was linked to road spending', the Productivity Commission (2014: 150) believed the best initial step in the reform process would be for each of the states and territories (and aggregations of local governments) to establish their own hypothecated road funds earmarked for road investment. It also argued that 'reform of direct road user charging is not a prerequisite for the adoption of the governance and institutional arrangements' it proposed. Nevertheless, in the same report, the Productivity Commission (2014: 141) recommended that 'governments should undertake pilot studies of (revenue neutral) direct road user pricing using vehicle telematics'. In short, the commission's report identified an idealised, efficient model of road user pricing and investment, but argued that, in the immediate term, interim steps could be taken towards enhancing the sustainability of the current system.

A more prescriptive advocacy discussion paper released by Infrastructure Partnerships Australia (2013) and prepared by Deloitte contrasted the existing funding framework with five other pricing models to compare their effectiveness. In the report entitled *Road Pricing and Transport Infrastructure Funding*, the alternatives considered were:

1. a cordon zone option for congestion charging (partial pricing in high-use facilities)
2. corridor-specific charging (partial pricing affecting national highways but all vehicles)
3. pricing charges for selected classes of vehicles on parts of the network
4. pricing for selected vehicles for the whole of the network
5. a universal model applying across the whole of the road network and incorporating all vehicles.

The report makes a strong case for the last model, called the 'universal road user charge model', applied across the entire road network. It is the only pricing model that generates additional funds for roads and meets the five analytical parameter challenges (it provides additional funding, covers road maintenance needs, charges the full allocation of costs, provides funding security and improves network performance).

The Deloitte report suggested there are three important features of this universal road user charge model. First, it would generate additional revenues to fund the network sustainably. Charges would be applied to road users 'based on time, distance, location and the mass of the vehicle using the road network' (Infrastructure Partnerships Australia 2013: 48). Second, it would entirely replace the existing charges applying to fuel and fixed access/registration charges, and possibly even compulsory insurance. These would all be abolished as unnecessary. Third, it proposed to hypothecate the funds raised from the road pricing model into a single fund earmarked for transport investments. Although this preferred model was credited with meeting the criteria of providing a secure and sustainable funding source into the future, elsewhere the report indicates that it costed the charges on a 'revenue-neutral' basis, 'meaning that the revenue of the new scheme would be equal to the current road-related revenues collected by federal and state governments' (Infrastructure Partnerships Australia 2013: 48). However, as noted above in the early parts of the report examining whether the current system is broken, the authors note that revenues from fuel excise are declining both in absolute terms and as a proportion of GDP; hence, rather than being entirely revenue-neutral, road user pricing would increase costs to motorists into the future over what they otherwise would be paying if fuel excise remained the principal source of revenue. Hence, to the extent that government dependence on fuel excise is decreasing as a proportion of total taxation receipts, user charging would replace this quantum with a source of revenues that could maintain the real magnitude of funding at present levels (or increase in the future).

The report acknowledges that such a road user charging scheme based on telematics was planned by The Netherlands Government for introduction between 2012 and 2016, but was scrapped in 2010 when the sponsoring coalition government (the fourth Christian Democratic Appeal government of Jan Peter Balkenende) broke down and subsequently lost office at the elections later that year. Legislation authorising the Dutch charging regime lapsed when the governing coalition collapsed in February 2010 and the eventual new minority government that emerged post election, led by the centre-right Prime Minister Mark Rutte (People's Party for Freedom and Democracy), indicated it would not proceed with a per kilometre road charge.

Whereas other reports tend to focus on the merits of adopting a user-based charging scheme but say little about the specifics of various funding models or how they will be implemented, the Deloitte discussion paper goes on to outline staged 'pathways to reform' and an implementation schedule. Implementation is based on incremental steps, beginning with the national harmonisation of registration fees and the adoption of a national registration regulator, reducing the fuel excise rate, hypothecating revenues from roads, the reform of road funding and governance arrangements, implementing user charges for major highways and mass distance, adjusting heavy vehicle charges to incorporate their impacts on the environment and other road users and introducing time-of-day differentiated charging regimes to manage acute congestion in peak periods.

A subsequent paper, produced by consultants Pricewaterhouse Coopers (PWC) for Infrastructure Australia, entitled *Modelling of Potential Policy Reforms*, has recently argued in relation to transport reform:

Federal, state and territory governments should commit to the full implementation of a heavy vehicle road charging structure in the next five years. This reform should include the removal of all existing registration and usage charges under the PayGo model and the introduction of supporting regulatory and investment frameworks ...

Federal, state and territory governments should also commit to the full implementation of a light vehicle road charging structure in the next ten years. This reform must include the removal of all existing inefficient taxes—including fuel excise and registration charges—and the development of supporting regulatory and investment frameworks. (Infrastructure Australia 2016: iii)

The PayGo system is a bureaucratic system run through the National Transport Commission that estimates an arbitrary percentage of costs (50 per cent) associated with heavy vehicle usage based on a three-year rolling set of estimates (involving some physical monitoring), with some urban and regional roads excluded from the calculations. This calculated figure is then applied through fixed vehicle registration fees to different classes of heavy vehicles. It forces heavy vehicle users to make some contribution for wear and tear, but is a very inexact levy, leading to calls from rail operators to introduce a more refined 'mass–distance–location' charging scheme. Rail operators are concerned that there is still a substantial cross-subsidisation of road haulage at the expense of rail freight carriers.

Moving away from the bureaucratic PayGo system, the PWC report calculated that the positive impact of the proposed reforms was estimated to be a productivity gain of 10 per cent for heavy vehicles from 2021 and a 15 per cent gain from the light vehicle reforms starting in 2028. Elsewhere in the report, PWC calculated that the net increase in GDP would equal $23.8 billion by 2031 and $34.8 billion by 2040 (Infrastructure Australia 2016: 47). Unlike earlier reform proposals that anticipated an ongoing mix of funding arrangements, the PWC proposal opted starkly for a direct user charging system to entirely replace the existing indiscriminate levies and charges, although it did not particularly stress the need for congestion charging in addition to user distance charging.

Immediate problems with the reform proposals

The main reform proposals involve not only a major change in the ways Australians pay for road transport, but also considerable institutional recalibration to make any proposed scheme viable. They also require the various governments to work together and honour commitments made about the way the system should work, and for the community to suspend their collective disbelief and instead trust governments to stand by commitments to the sector. As of mid-2017, the Commonwealth Government had not made any firm decision on road funding reform, although the Minister for Urban Infrastructure, Paul Fletcher, indicated in a ministerial statement to Parliament (in December 2015) that the government would accelerate work with the states and territories to consider options to 'introduce cost-reflective road pricing for all vehicles'. Nevertheless, the author understands that many policy departments of the federal government are yet to sign on to the proposed reform agenda—not least Treasury, Finance, Prime Minister and Cabinet, Social Services and Human Services, Agriculture, Forestry and Fisheries, Regional Development and Northern Australia. Moreover, no state or territory government has committed to a user charging system despite most likely being the main beneficiaries of such a system, and indeed many have explicitly ruled out such a system. Some prominent commentators, such as Marion Terrill, have described the reform options as arousing 'diabolical politics' that will in all likelihood scuttle the prospects of any beneficial scheme producing optimal results.

I outline the main sticking points to overcome in any user charging reform proposal.

Too many contending schemes?

One of the challenges for government policymakers is that there are many different and potentially rival proposals—in scope, ambition and application—although most are heading in similar directions to increase user charging. This is not an unfamiliar story in other policy areas. The best way to proceed for governments in such circumstances is for them to be as clear as possible in their (sometimes competing) objectives, identify which options best address those objectives or which are politically feasible and then prioritise the reforms (noting that some reforms can be complementary) and undertake validation checks before embarking on implementation. Only by being so clear and focused will governments stand any chance of gaining interjurisdictional agreement and community acceptance of the proposed options.

Some proposed schemes currently on the table are very explicit about the link between charging regimes and investment funding arrangements, while others leave such topics to future exigencies—leaving administrative arrangements ambiguous even though they are concerned to advocate for more resources to the network. Some pooling of collected user charge funds would create an investment potential but could get mired in the Lasswellian politics of 'who gets what, when and where'. However, those interested only in congestion charges to rationalise usage at peak times or charge for access to CBD areas tend to focus on preventive measures (penalty charges for travelling in peak times) and far less on hypothecated reinvestment in road infrastructure. Some reform proposals seek a complete system overhaul over a relatively short period, while others recommend trials and pilot programs to test the efficacy of reform models.

The upshot of having these contending models is that governments need to commission their various agencies to develop a coherent reform agenda based on clearly articulated objectives relating to the efficient use of the road network and pricing that delivers the appropriate supportive incentives. An incremental approach may be wisest, perhaps coordinated through COAG or a multijurisdictional interdepartmental committee structure. In the absence of such a multiparty agreement over the adoption of a coherent reform agenda, it is unlikely any government alone will decide to go ahead, meaning valuable time will be wasted and implementation will be stalled.

Shifting to a user pricing regime?

A crucial issue for governments to resolve will be how to justifiably set pricing for the provision of a service that is largely a monopoly provision, whether provided directly by Australian governments or leased in various forms to private toll road operators. Any declared user charging 'price' is liable to attract the criticism that it is inherently arbitrary, administratively determined and compulsorily imposed. Given governments collectively run the road system and would be involved in setting the price signals (even if an independent economic regulator was established), there are twin dangers in overpricing and/or inflexible pricing. Bureaucrats are not always responsive to markets. If history is to be believed and bearing in mind previous traditions of managing public infrastructure, governments are likely to lay down a specific charging regime and concentrate on imposing it, while only occasionally assessing whether it achieves the right balance between sociopolitical objectives and market realities.

One proposal put forward by some infrastructure planners is for governments to set indicative revenue targets equal not only to all existing road-related investment, but also to the strategic priorities ahead. If taken to its logical conclusion—and any proposed user charging funding model was based on assessed future need—it would imply that road pricing would be 'supply driven' (geared to the desired investment plans) rather than 'demand driven' by consumers or focused on demand management. This would mean that today's drivers would cross-subsidise future generations in their enjoyment of the road network. Given the road system is largely a monopolistic public utility, a very real question we need to ask is how much we hope or intend to raise looking into the future (see below). In part, this problem could be overcome by the use of borrowings to finance the investment plans (as occurs presently with many major road and infrastructural projects), with the debt serviced and the principal repaid by the users of the day over the effective life of the investment.

In determining a pricing regime, governments also need to establish what charges will be included in the pricing model. For instance, are governments likely to impose only the direct charges, such as for the distance travelled, routes taken, the vehicle size or load carried, or are we going to include charges for other impacts (or 'externalities'), such as carbon dioxide emissions, traffic accidents, policing and emergency services, traffic management or even noise and air pollution? The Henry review suggested such costs be controlled by regulation and linked into a system-wide carbon pollution reduction scheme, taken from general revenue or even met by better insurance premiums.

Advances in technology can provide some of the answers and deal with some of the difficulties. Technologies such as telematics now allow us to be sophisticated with vehicle monitoring (route and distance) and allow variations in charging regimes, so it is not difficult to envisage that different rates of charging can apply for regional Australians driving on rural roads where there is no congestion, or discounted rates for non-metropolitan zones. However, even quiet rural roads cannot be provided free to farming or mining communities, despite these constituencies being politically well connected and their parliamentary representatives often not supporting user charging schemes. Rural roads are generally not built as well as urban freeways and need repeated repair work. And, if smaller but significant 'C class' roads are exempt (to use the classification system used in some states), this may create perverse incentives for heavy vehicles carrying freight to use these sealed roads to evade charges. Complicated equity considerations will dominate these discussions—with as yet no real consensus nationwide as to what is fair, what is appropriate, how much concessionary groups should contribute, relative charges for different users or for different roads, and so on.

Historically, in imposing fixed vehicle registration fees and other charges, some state governments argued that a flat fee was equitable, in that if a motorist or consumer chose to drive a particular vehicle they would pay the same rate as another. However, states separately set these fixed but discretionary fees according to different criteria, creating a veritable mishmash of charging regimes and levied matrices. For instance, as of 2015, according to the various state and territory government websites, there was considerable variation in registration prices for an average motor vehicle, ranging from $1,120 per annum in the Australian Capital Territory to only $608 in Tasmania. New South Wales charged owners $904, whereas Victoria charged $787. Furthermore, many states use these fixed-charge systems to deliver 'community service obligations' and allow discounts for pensioners or seniors, carers or the disabled or in some cases to fix charges at different rates between city and country drivers.

A single independent charging institution and investment planner: Wishing away federalism?

Despite the hopes of some state parliamentary committees, it would be very difficult to operate coherent multiple road pricing schemes at the subnational level. The main reasons weighing against this option are to avoid spillover effects, reduce transaction costs and contain administrative costs and leakages, especially between separate charging systems given the high degree of interstate mobility. For instance, if one state removed entirely its registration fees and adopted a user pricing mechanism, but another state did not and retained its registration fees, it would be possible to register for free in the first state and yet drive for free in the second state.[3]

---

3   Admittedly, there is a degree of leakage under the present vehicle registration system, with people and firms able to register in the jurisdiction with the cheapest level of fees (for example, hire car companies or people with multiple addresses). For instance, many people who live in Canberra seem to drive vehicles with cheaper NSW registration plates.

In recognition of this circumstance, many reform advocates have suggested—sensibly perhaps—the establishment of a single national institution to lead road charging (often called the 'single national economic regulator'). They recommend that (as a minimum) a national body would develop consistent principles (possibly approved by a ministerial council) that would apply nationwide, perhaps deliver competitive neutrality between different transport sectors (road, rail, shipping) and allow a single collection agency to administer the scheme. Such a body (were governments to empower it) *could* perform many other functions, such as establishing the rates of charging and set fees, collecting and distributing the revenues collected and making infrastructural decisions that were aligned with network needs and productivity considerations. However, as discussed later in this chapter, it is not necessary for a national body that administers the pricing regulation and/or revenue collection to be the same one that evaluates and recommends to ministers the priorities for road funding.

Two distinct models for a single national economic regulator suggest themselves, although neither is without its own political problems of implementation. First, the states collectively could agree to 'go it alone' and set up a coordinated interstate body (a bottom-up initiative) with the same set of charging and congestion rates. Their immediate problems would be how to implement consistent user charges across Australia and how to convince the Commonwealth Government to withdraw from excise taxation on fuels (or gain some agreement on a joint partial funding model, which would erode the integrity of the user charging scheme). A similar bottom-up model is being rolled out by many of the states in the area of e-health patient records compiled and accessible by doctors, pharmacists and eventually hospitals, and in direct opposition to the Commonwealth's bungled attempted imposition of its flawed national MyHealth initiative, which was widely seen as too time-consuming, likely to be punitive and not useful for patient care.

Second, a single national economic regulator could be established involving the Commonwealth and the states and territories (and even local governments as well) to administer the user charging regime. Presumably, this mooted national body would be an independent one established under intergovernmental agreement. But would the Commonwealth, either by decree or by stealth, seek to 'control' this body, as some consider has happened with other intergovernmental entities, or would the states exert their own control of it and, if so, how would divergent state interests be mediated? It would be a challenge to design a governance structure for a national economic regulator responsible for user charging, roads funding and infrastructure prioritising, or even for each of those functions separately. The danger of having a national planning body that was dominated by state interests would be that national visions and priorities would be surrendered to parochial concerns of the major states, especially given the non-standardised or differential election cycles.

Moreover, if a nationally consistent scheme was adopted, what would be expected of the Commonwealth? Would the Commonwealth want to become more involved in frontline/operational transport management in metropolitan or regional areas, and does it have the capabilities and local knowledge to do so? There are real question marks over the issue of respective capabilities, a history of institutional distrust and zero-sum politics, notwithstanding the promotion of the subsidiary principle in some quarters.

Who would decide priorities for strategic infrastructural investment and priority maintenance?

States might be coaxed to agree with the logic of having a single entity to administer the charging and receipt of revenues, but states are unlikely to want it to determine infrastructural priorities. They would in all likelihood insist on a formulaic share-of-revenue model (similar to many existing arrangements under Section 96 funding agreements, but unlike the regularly contested goods and services tax (GST), which has funded states on an assessment of expenditure need and revenue capacity relative to the national average). Such a formulaic sharing model (distributed on a per capita basis or some other criteria that could be agreed on) in essence would be non-strategic, unresponsive to market demands or behavioural changes and lock in funding where it may continue to be inefficient.

Would state and territory governments, in particular, be prepared seriously to give up the power to make politically sensitive (and politically driven) decisions to commission new roads, prioritise network improvements and determine the precedence of road maintenance plans? While there are concerns that insufficient funds are directed to road building, spending on roads remains an important form of pork-barrelling, especially between politicians and the citizenry when there are relatively limited opportunities for delivering local largesse. There is much electoral kudos at stake and enormous local lobbying about road improvements. It seems unlikely that Australian jurisdictions will hand the power to determine road priorities over to an independent body or a national funding body or even allow a national body to 'pick and choose' from a prepared list of intended projects. However, as noted above, the functions of road pricing regulation and road investment analysis need not coexist.

Hypothecating the revenues raised, establishing locked boxes for infrastructure?

It is doubtful a national road user charging scheme could work optimally without some form of hypothecation, whether Australia went straight to a hypothecated model or moved towards it in stages. Hypothecated funding for the network would be the obverse of the pricing side of the equation. Logically, all funds raised from road transport (congestion charges or user charges) ought to be ploughed back into improvements to the road network and ought to *be seen* to be ploughed back by fee-paying road consumers. There is far better public acceptance of revenue-generating regimes that tie the revenues raised back to a definite worthwhile purpose. Arguably, roads are better suited to this kind of cost-recovery regime involving hypothecation than other areas of public policy—for instance, tying hospital expenditure (driven by the health needs of the community) to the revenue generated from a national lottery (driven by the propensity of some people to gamble).

To date, a number of state governments have used limited hypothecation instruments for traffic fine revenue to be tied to road safety programs (New South Wales, Victoria, Queensland, South Australia and Western Australia). For instance, the NSW Government (at the Auditor-General's recommendation) has put a toe into the water of hypothecation by establishing the Community Road Safety Fund in 2013, into which all traffic fines for speed camera and red-light camera offences are deposited (approximately $137 million per annum when the fund was established). These hypothecated funds are directed not particularly to investments in roads, but to road safety, including the enforcement of road rules by police and road safety engineers; and, at the time of its establishment, these fines were estimated to cover approximately half of the road safety costs of the state government (budgeted at $231 million in 2011–12, while the cost of speed-related crashes was more than $1.7 billion annually).

It must be acknowledged that there is much opposition to hypothecation in Australia. Such schemes can be seen as an arbitrary compartmentalisation of budgets, which can then put artificial constraints on budgetary flexibility and allocative efficiency—and perhaps limit the potential of increasing funds to pressing priorities. Under hypothecated conditions, infrastructure planners would have, in effect, a locked box to spend on projects irrespective of competing priorities within transport funding or with societal issues such as health and aged care. Such an approach equally attempts to defy political logics, economic cycles and planning sequences. A survey of road funding since 1990 conducted by the Parliamentary Library (Webb 2000: i) argued against hypothecation by suggesting:

> Arguments that more of the revenue raised from motor vehicle taxes should be earmarked (hypothecated) for spending on roads are questionable. The level of Commonwealth road funding is determined in the overall budget context without reference to the revenue raised from particular taxes, and expenditure on roads competes with other expenditures. The House of Representatives Standing Committee has recommended that the hypothecation provisions in the Australian Land Transport Development Act 1988 be removed to end the notion of a link between fuel excise revenue and the level of road funding.

This classical attack on hypothecation is premised on the notion that all taxation collected from various sources should go to general consolidated revenue so that spending plans 'compete with other expenditures'. This is separate from the aforementioned approach of user paying, whereby user charges are applied for certain forms of public provision to meet the costs of delivering those services to the community. Such user charging models are in fact an efficient way of harnessing market forces to ensure demand recognises the costs of supply, and that consumers are able to allocate their funding to areas of highest value to them.

Complex intergovernmental aspects?

Not surprisingly, road pricing initiatives globally have typically taken place in unitary systems (or city-states) where the national government has the constitutional power to impose the scheme. Federations are more problematic, although Germany has had a heavy vehicle toll on federal highways since 2005. Incentives/disincentives for states to join a national road pricing scheme have already been mentioned above, but other challenging intergovernmental dimensions are likely to affect any implementation of a pricing regime. At the local level, where there are minimal opportunities for leakage, states with significant congestion problems would be able to vary congestion charges to suit local conditions (or, alternatively, to 'sweat' infrastructure outside peak-hour commuting times). To make a national system work, states may have to either introduce common template legislation empowering such a body or refer powers to the Commonwealth so that the constitutionality of any proposed reform would withstand legal challenge by a disgruntled jurisdiction or constituency. Were the states to choose to refer their powers there remains legal uncertainty about whether they can ever reclaim those powers.

Likely problems with undertaking tax trade-offs and the abolition of existing charges and fees

To date, most of the modelling on road pricing has come from economic theory positing a perfect world of rational action. In practice, it is unlikely any level of government will behave altruistically or surrender powers or revenue instruments at its disposal. Assumptions that moving to a new system based on the introduction of a pricing mechanism dependent on actual usage (and one that is able to affect behavioural change) will lead to a complete transformation of road funding are not credible. Political economy will come to the fore. There is also the assumption that a pure pricing model does not need to rely on other existing levies and blunt charges to work effectively (and that any retention of fixed levies would distort consumer decisions; Henry et al. 2010: 398–9).

Hence, we see assertions bandied around that when the new charging regime is introduced the raft of existing levies will be abolished at the outset of the transition phase or phased out over a limited period. Many of the reformist reports naively make the assumption in their cost–benefit calculations that the existing state taxes and levies would be entirely repealed as the new system gets under way. In these modelling calculations, the fixed charges that states and territories impose on vehicle owners would be abolished, as could compulsory third-party insurance rates, which could be included in and priced into the direct charging regime. States would effectively be asked to give up certain instruments of taxation, leaving them with an even narrower tax base, exacerbating vertical fiscal imbalance issues and facing the prospect of never getting such taxation instruments back again. Surrendering such inefficient and irritant fixed-based taxes in exchange for a generic and largely non-discriminatory national system would require a huge leap of faith by subnational governments, and only one or two of these jurisdictions need to object or refuse to participate for the system to be threatened. It is more likely that states and territories will agree to decrease these levied fixed charges but not abolish them entirely.

While it is true that many of the fixed levies imposed by states and territories are inefficient and irritating, they can nevertheless be manipulated for political gain/social engineering. States can use their own discretion to increase registration fees and give concessions to selected constituencies for electoral reasons. It is highly unlikely states and territories will entirely abolish vehicle registration charges, stamp duties, charges for number plates, drivers' licences, compulsory third-party insurance or even vehicle safety checks and roadworthy certificates. This is despite the fact that these items could all be incorporated and covered through a national pricing mechanism that was geared more towards actual usage.

Similarly, the Commonwealth enjoys the undisputed constitutional power to levy and collect fuel excise. It is unlikely to surrender this power or abolish the excise duty entirely. Even if a road pricing scheme comes into play, technically replacing the need for excise entirely (in that distance usage is captured within the pricing), it would be in the Commonwealth's interest to retain some excise charge. More than likely, the Commonwealth will redefine the nature of the excise charge so it is able to retain some component of the existing levy. For instance, currently, fuel excise is taxed to provide a funding source for roads (a partial earmarking or hypothecation), but if roads were to be funded directly through revenues raised entirely through user charges, the Commonwealth could still insist on collecting some fuel excise by redefining the excise tax as a means to capture the other negative externalities (such as pollution or depletion of a non-renewable resource).

The Henry review of taxation tackled this issue when it argued that 'fuel tax and other transport taxes are not an efficient or equitable means of financing general government expenditure' (Henry et al. 2010: 375 and E3-1). However, the Productivity Commission (2017: 1–2) has argued the fuel tax credit enjoyed by off-road mining and farming sectors is:

> not considered assistance as the excise tax on fuel is purported to be a mechanism to pay for roads, which are not used by those receiving the fuel rebate. Should roads be generally priced, as discussed in the Commission's Public Infrastructure [Productivity Commission 2014], the taxation of fuel would change, perhaps towards a recognition of the negative externalities of fuel consumption. A diesel fuel rebate under those conditions would constitute assistance.

Hence, by redefining fuel excise in economic terminology, the Commonwealth would claim ground to retain some portion of that tax even though it is not regarded as appropriate for general taxation purposes. Moreover, in addition to the complex interests around paying for road use, changes to the existing fuel excise may affect off-road vehicle users, bringing powerful mining and farming interests into conflict with the aims of the road pricing policy.

A parallel case on which to reflect involves the introduction of the GST in 2000. The Commonwealth managed to convince the subnational governments in 1999–2000 to abolish a list of inefficient taxes as part of the adoption of the broad-based GST, arguing that the replacement funds generated by the GST would then be transferred to these jurisdictions. Seventeen years later, however, many of these irritant state taxes are still in place. States dragged the chain or simply refused to repeal these duties and fixed taxes. This example suggests the states and territories would be reluctant to vacate the road vehicle/driver registration processes if a national universal charging regime were imposed. Most observers would conclude from history that they would be inclined to retain some or all of these charges, although perhaps levied at a reduced rate.

Sceptics could be forgiven for concluding that, aside from some potentially better management of our road transport network, one of the principal objectives of road pricing reform is to seek an increase in funding going to roads while pretending that motorists will not pay more. Retaining the existing array of state-based levies while introducing a full-cost user-based pricing mechanism would constitute a sleight of hand. The Productivity Commission (2014: 151) mentioned this when it talked of the 'widespread fear among motorists that they would be worse off'.

Transitional arrangements?

Another problematic issue to consider is the transitional arrangements necessary to move from the existing overly complex and multi-actor system of road charging to one of universal road user charging. Ideally, any pricing scheme should be phased in over time, but this will weaken the impact of the price signals and expected behavioural responses. Would states and territories move as one and dismantle their various fixed fee structures according to an agreed uniform schedule? If not, various users in those jurisdictions that attempt to hold on to former levies will face a 'double whammy' until the rates eventually fall.

There are other transitional complications such as what to do with the existing toll road and tunnel facilities, many of which are governed by long-term operational contracts as part of public–private partnerships (PPP) arrangements. Toll prices are likely to remain far higher than a comparable systemic user charge for road usage mainly because toll charges are set to cover the investment costs amortised over a certain period, not principally to manage demand and cover usage. Moreover, toll prices tend to be standardised according to the class of vehicle, not variable subject to congestion levels (although in theory they could be made more volume sensitive). Can toll operations be included in a seamless pricing regime, while still identifying the necessary payments and forwarding these to the operators? Alternatively, can toll roads fall back into the system of public provision and be priced according to usage and congestion, and presumably with the operators given compensation for their loss of business?

Future issues?

A central question for pricing advocates to answer is whether pricing will replace the existing quantum of funds that currently flows through the system (conforming to principles of 'budget neutrality') or provide sufficient funds to cover the entire costs of running the road system (to eliminate any cross-subsidisation from general revenue)? Or, alternatively, are we hoping to raise increased funds to invest in system upgrades and enhanced infrastructure into the future? These matters need to be addressed in the process of setting clear objectives and preferred options.

An interesting conundrum to contemplate is that Australia, like many other parts of the world, may not remain wedded to individual car transportation into the future. Car usage may decline, especially if investments in rapid public transport accelerate and cities consolidate their population density rather than continue the previous pattern of urban sprawl. Working from home or from centres closer to one's residence may reduce the necessity for employees and others to commute. The increasing availability of online services and information accessibility will lessen the need to travel to one specific place to receive such benefits. Road network planners will have to consider what to do if usage begins to drop dramatically (and already we have evidence that today's motorists are driving less than before, making fewer trips and consuming less petrol than previously). Even a small user charge in monetary terms may encourage motorists to combine trips (opting for fewer, multipurpose trips) and discourage them from making optional or non-imperative trips. Under such circumstances, how would a national economic regulator of roads respond? Would an efficient road charging regime see prices increase if usage declined, to make up for the shortfall in required estimated revenues, or would prices decrease, reflecting less wear and tear and less demand for road transport? And, if prices were to rise to cover revenue shortfalls, would this further discourage motorists, thus exacerbating the problems? Moreover, if higher volumes of heavy freight were transferred from roads to rail under a policy of competitive neutrality, how would the prices charged for heavy vehicle usage respond?

While moving to a cost-recovery system responding to market signals and demand may make much sense in public policy terms, there remain many areas of unpredictability and future unknowables. Adopting such market mechanisms may enable more flexible management of the transport network into the future, but markets are themselves imperfect and can also have perverse logics and consequences. These issues will have to be sensitively managed with much analytical foresight and astute judgement. There is already some recognition of this dilemma in the published reports reviewed in this chapter, with many calling for root and branch reviews and systemic evaluations to be conducted on a regular basis. Road transport reform remains a pressing imperative for governments at all levels of Australian politics and of all political persuasions. Currently, there are many options for market reform already on the table, but not all have met with rapturous applause or been embraced by the various jurisdictions around Australia. In all likelihood, the magnitude of change in road transport that will occur in the future will be truly transformational and will revolutionise the present broken system for all time; the challenges ahead are formidable and the politics may well be 'diabolical', but we cannot afford to not 'get it right' as we go forward.

References

Australasian Railways Association. (2010). *Road Pricing Reforms in Australia*. Sydney: Australasian Railways Association.

Fletcher, P. (2015). Ministerial statement on road pricing, 2 December. Canberra: Parliament of Australia.

Graham, P. W. and Reedman, L. J. (2015). *Projecting future road transport revenues 2015–2050*. Report for the National Transport Commission. Melbourne: CSIRO. Available from: www.ntc.gov.au/Media/Reports/(68BBFA97-3FAF-4266-A478-5ED625F7559E).pdf

Henry, K., Harmer, J., Piggott, J., Ridout, H. and Smith, G. (2010). *Australia's Future Tax System: Report to the Treasurer, Detailed Analysis Volume 2*. Canberra: Commonwealth of Australia.

Infrastructure Australia. (2013). *National Infrastructure Plan*. June. Canberra: Infrastructure Australia.

Infrastructure Australia. (2016). *Modelling of Potential Policy Reforms*. PWC report to Infrastructure Australia, February. Canberra: Infrastructure Australia.

Infrastructure Partnerships Australia. (2013). *Road Pricing and Transport Infrastructure Funding: Reform Pathways for Australia*. Sydney: Deloitte/Infrastructure Partnerships Australia.

National Transport Commission. (2012). *Heavy Vehicles Charges 2012–13*. Canberra: National Transport Commission.

Productivity Commission. (2014). *Public Infrastructure*. Canberra: Productivity Commission.

Productivity Commission. (2017). *Trade & Assistance Review, 2015–16*. Canberra: Productivity Commission. Available from: www.pc.gov.au/research/ongoing/trade-assistance/2015-16/trade-assistance-review-2015-16.pdf

Road Safety Parliamentary Committee. (2010). *Inquiry into Federal–State Road Funding Arrangements*. Melbourne: Parliament of Victoria.

Saulwick, J. (2014). Fix NSW transport: Road access pricing. *Sydney Morning Herald*, 24 September.

Terrill, M. and Emslie, O. (2016). Road user charging belongs on the political agenda as the best answer for congestion management. *The Conversation*, 12 September.

Terrill, M., Emslie, O. and Coates, B. (2016). *Roads to Riches: Better Transport Investment*. Melbourne: Grattan Institute.

Webb, R. (2000). *Commonwealth Road Funding since 1990*. Research Paper No. 13 1999–2000. Canberra: Department of the Parliamentary Library. Available from: www.aph.gov.au/binaries/library/pubs/rp/1999-2000/2000rp13.pdf

www.ingramcontent.com/pod-product-compliance
Lightning Source LLC
Chambersburg PA
CBHW050811270326
41926CB00052B/4645